BEYOND THE

The inside story of how 9 everyday
investors found financial freedom through
property

ISBN-10: 1494783916

ISBN-13: 978-1494783914

Also by Rob Dix:

Property Investment for Beginners

(Find out more at propertygeek.net/beginners)

Contents

His move across the country looked like a whim, but Gavin's growing empire is actually the phase 1 of an ambitious 25-year plan.

Kim Stones is a problem-solver, and his inventive solutions allowed him to succeed when he could have lost absolutely everything.

Mat didn't know what "yield" meant, yet he still had the confidence to buy 30 properties in 18 months – then repeat the process abroad.

Property nearly ruined her, but it saved her too – and introduced her to a bizarre new social circle.

Introduction

When you want to know how to do something, here's what you should do: buy lunch for someone who's already doing it. I'm a property investor and I want to be as successful as possible, so over the course of 2012 and 2013 I approached nine people and offered to do exactly that.

Funnily enough, property investors don't seem to eat – which made the venture even more cost-effective. Instead we drove hundreds of miles together, viewed tens of their own houses and those they were considering buying, and drank inadvisable amounts of McDonald's coffee.

I already knew that there was no single way of being successful in property, which is why I spoke to nine different investors – and I could have spoken to many more without encountering the same method twice.

I also took a deliberately broad definition of "success". To me, "success" doesn't mean making as much money as possible whatever the cost. Instead, "success" is about achieving a lifestyle that's satisfying, sustainable and independent. Sometimes that comes with the trappings of material wealth, but not always.

The stories are fascinating in their own right, given that my interviewees have built up great wealth by eschewing the 9-to-5, learning as they go, and weathering at least one major recession that could have wiped them out. More than just being of human interest though, I wanted this book to help new and aspiring investors to decide which route to go down. For that reason I've focused not just on what happened, but what my interviewees' lifestyles are like now.

So if you're reading this book purely for enjoyment, I hope the stories entertain you. But if you're also looking for pointers for your own investments, there are plenty. I discuss some of the recurring themes in the conclusion, but otherwise it's up to you to draw your own lessons: some people will have made a lot of money but ended up with a lifestyle you wouldn't want, whereas other approaches might seem ideally suited to your own skills and preferences. You can use the stories to gather new ideas, challenge your existing views and fuel future research and decisions.

Research methods

I found my interviewees through personal connections, recommendations and posts on several property message boards. I wanted to cover as many different strategies as possible – from standard buy-to-let to more exotic tools like lease options – and to talk to people in many parts of the country with very different property and tenant profiles. I couldn't possibly hope to cover every possible angle, but I did the best that I could.

My only definite criterion for inclusion was that they had been actively investing in the last few years. Many people have built up big portfolios using methods that aren't possible now, so have been sitting back since the credit crunch. Their stories would have been interesting, but of limited use to people looking for investment pointers in the current climate. For the same reason, I excluded anyone who started with an unusually large amount of capital, either earned or inherited.

All of the interviewees were offered anonymity, but most declined. Some of them are very visible in the property investment community – some even offering courses or other services to other investors – but I satisfied myself that commercial gain wasn't a motive for them to take part. Other interviewees have never spoken publicly, blogged or even posted on a message board before.

I have conducted some background research on the interviewees using publicly available data, but I don't claim to have fact-checked every detail of their stories. There may be inaccuracies and omissions, but I feel confident that any such errors will be purely accidental, and won't materially affect the lessons contained in their stories.

It is also likely that my sample of interviewees is biased through self-selection, luck, survivorship, or anything else you can think of. This isn't an academic study – just a collection of stories from which you're free to take whatever you wish.

You'll probably end up liking most of the investors after reading their stories, but that's not because they had copy approval over what I wrote about them. I showed each of them a draft of my chapter to correct factual errors in what they said or how I transcribed it, but all the conclusions and interpretations are wholly my own. If they come across as a likeable bunch, it's just because I liked them. They were all generous enough to spend at least three hours with me telling me their stories, and you would be happy to be seated opposite any one of them at a dinner party.

So, enjoy the next nine chapters in the company of these successful, self-motivated and thoughtful individuals. Enjoy their stories as stories, and see what pointers and lessons you can take to refine your own direction in property investment. At the end, I'll discuss some of the main themes that popped out at me from our conversations, and you'll also find a glossary of common investment jargon. If there are any terms you don't understand as the stories unfold, look there for simple explanations.

Onwards!

Rob

Mark Alexander

"If the apocalypse happens, property prices halve, interest rates double and all your boilers break down at once...would you rather have been saving £100 each month, or have £25,000 in the bank?"

When Mark picks me up from the station in his Jaguar XJ, it's clear he's come a long way from his teenage years in Wolverhampton – where he left school early, worked in a factory and danced in a nightclub at weekends to make a bit of extra money.

But although Mark built up a huge property portfolio and appears to have all the trappings of wealth, it's far from a simple rags-to-riches tale: along the way he had times when he couldn't afford to feed his daughter, and was once forced to lay off hundreds of staff and shut down his business just a year after receiving an offer to sell it for millions.

As he readily admits, accumulating a large property portfolio was "pure ego". But over time Mark became very interested in and passionate about property itself – rather than just the money – and he began to develop deeply contrarian ideas about financing and management that have allowed him to run a highly profitable, hands-off portfolio that's spread all over the country. Now, having lived the high life off his rental income, all he wants to do is tour Europe in a caravan...if he can only get his wife to agree.

Growing up

Mark grew up into a working-class family in Wolverhampton, with no particular exposure to property: his parents were the first in the family to own their own home rather than live in a council house.

He left school at 16, by which time he'd already spent two years with a very unusual part-time job for a white kid from the Midlands in late 1970s: breakdancing in local nightclubs. "My mate Lee spent some time in Brooklyn and Harlem and saw all this acrobatic dancing that there wasn't a name for at the time. He came back and said 'This will help us pull the girls!' It was only later, in 1983, that the film *Breakdance* came out and everyone started getting into it, and suddenly we had all these offers to dance in clubs. One of our regular gigs was at an R'n'B club in the middle of Birmingham: everyone was black, and we were two 15-year-old white kids there purely for entertainment purposes. We thought we were going to get lynched, but the girls thought it was the cutest thing ever!"

After leaving school Mark moved to King's Lynn, but kept up the breakdancing – driving back to Birmingham at weekends on his 125cc motorcycle. He bounced between various YTS courses, training as a butcher before eventually finding a job working in a factory. Then in 1987, when Mark was 19, Lee drove over in a brand new car. He said that he'd earned it by selling life insurance, and recruited Mark into the business.

Now with better prospects, Mark's parents convinced him to buy his first property: a two-up two-down mid-terrace in King's Lynn. Property prices were rocketing, and they were concerned that if he didn't buy soon he'd never get onto the housing ladder.

While getting started in the insurance business, Mark continued working a full time split shift in a factory – where he met a woman who became his first client, and also his first wife. "She bought a £40-a-month savings plan off me – best investment she ever made!"

Pushed to the brink

In 1989, Mark was headhunted by Citibank and started dealing in mortgages as well as life insurance. Before long though, Citibank started to gradually withdraw from the UK market. With the prospect of losing their jobs, Mark and a colleague decided to jump before they were pushed; they set up their own commercial finance business where they arranged mortgages for hotels, restaurants, offices and nursing homes.

Mark sold his small house, and together he and his wife moved into a three-bedroom detached bungalow in Norwich. It wasn't long before Mark realised they could no longer afford it: interest rates had shot up to the point that they couldn't pay the mortgage, and prices had crashed so they couldn't sell it either. They rented the bungalow out and moved into a tiny flat, allowing them to pay their own living costs while still subsidising their mortgage.

With interest rates spiking and the economy struggling, Mark found that his new company was doing most of its business with companies that were trying to raise finance to avoid going under. Although it was a tough time for the country in general, it was a golden learning opportunity for Mark: he was able to observe the companies they were able to save and those that became insolvent, and he started to build ideas about the reasons for the differences between the two.

"It started becoming very clear to me that it was the people and businesses without cash that were going under: those who *had* cash were taking advantage of the lower prices to quickly build very big property portfolios. I desperately wanted to emulate the successful people, and having cash in the bank has been a core part of my strategy ever since."

But building his empire would have to wait, because Mark's business was struggling to survive in the depressed early 90s economy. "When I left Citibank I was earning £38,000 – a lot of money back then – and was the original yuppie with my giant phone and Filofax. The next year, running my own business, me and my business partner earned £6,000 between us."

He was still living in a rented flat, had racked up £12,000 in personal debt, and had a further £12,000 debt that was being guaranteed by his parents. Mark was struggling.

"It was bloody awful. When my daughter was born in 1992, we couldn't afford to feed her so we had to keep 'popping in' on different family members for her meals. I wanted to declare bankruptcy: I had all this debt, I was working with all these insolvent businesses, I was in negative equity on my house and I was paying a mortgage with a 15% interest rate…but I couldn't go bankrupt or I'd pull my parents under with me. The only way out was to keep going."

Through all of this though, Mark had his eye on the successful investors who were taking full advantage of the downturn. "There was this one guy who bought 700 houses in 1992. He was buying them for £25,000, spending £5,000, and they were worth £40,000– £50,000 so he'd either sell them for a profit or refinance at 75% to get his money back out. He was a machine: he was making so much money, and I knew that I could do the same."

"Everyone I knew I'd ask to lend me money: 'Will you lend me £100k? No? How about £50,000? £10,000? Just £1,000 then?' But everyone could see that I was struggling, so they weren't interested. I'd just have to somehow save up on my own."

His first flat

Mark's goal was to save £10,000: enough for a deposit on a small flat in Norwich, plus the associated buying and refurbishment costs. Eventually, after years of watching the numbers in his bank account grow painfully slowly, in 1996 he reached the magic figure.

"When I finally had that £10,000, it was worth as much as £10 million would be to me now – so it was the scariest thing in the world to immediately take it out of the building society and invest it in property. It was like winning the lottery one week and being forced to spend it all on lottery tickets again the following Saturday."

Scary as it was, Mark had had years to research his first investment, and he'd developed a strong idea of what he wanted. He calculated his budget to be £20,000, based on putting in a £5,000 deposit and getting a 75% mortgage – which would leave him with £1,500 for refurbishment and costs, with a £3,500 margin of safety. "I needed some margin in case interest rates shot up again. Also, property prices were still in the doldrums; I was only operating on a hunch that prices would go up again."

Mark couldn't afford a house in an area of town that would be easy to rent, so he gravitated towards flats – which appealed because of the lower maintenance they'd require. His next decision was whether to buy an upstairs or downstairs flat: he knew that elderly people and young families with babies would prefer the ground floor, but from talking to other landlords he'd learnt that damp and security were both issues with ground-floor flats. He decided on first-floor flats, which would be likely to appeal to young working tenants, so he started looking at locations on the main bus routes into town and the local industrial estates.

After visiting every estate agent in town ("There was no Rightmove back then!"), Mark narrowed his search down to three flats – all of which were slightly above his budget. He put in offers of £19,000 for all three, and all of them were refused. He didn't dare to raise his offer and lose the cushion of his few thousand left in the bank, so he stuck to his guns – and soon one of the vendors changed their mind and agreed to his straightforward, chain-free offer. Mark was finally a property investor.

Mark rented out the flat for £325 per month, which made him "a nice little profit" even though the only mortgage he could secure at the time was at a 9% interest rate on a 15-year repayment basis.

But almost immediately, something was about to happen that would completely transform Mark's business and his property investment strategy beyond all recognition.

Buy-to-let is born

At the same time that Mark was buying his long-awaited first flat, the Association of Residential Letting Agents (ARLA) was coining the term "buy-to-let". With the aim of creating more buyers for the private rental sector, ARLA persuaded lenders to give out buy-to-let mortgages on almost the same terms as residential mortgages – rather than the onerous commercial terms that buyers had hitherto needed to comply with.

"Their argument was that instead of giving 100% mortgages to high-risk 21-year-olds, just add a 1% premium to the interest rate and give 75% interest-only mortgages to their parents to buy an investment property. The risks would be lower, and it'd be more commercially viable."

The scheme was more popular than anyone could have imagined: there were 150,000 enquiries in the first two weeks, and this created an opportunity for Mark's struggling mortgage business.

"The letting agents suddenly had their offices full of people who believed that the property market was turning, and they were saying 'Hang on a minute, we're not mortgage brokers – we can help you once you've bought it, but we can't help you with the finance.' So I went around all the ARLA agents and said that if they sent all their enquiries to us, we'd do the mortgages and give them a commission."

Mark's business suddenly had a steady supply of customers, and the market conditions helped him quickly scale up his staff to serve them too. "Banks had been busy laying people off, so we had all these former commercial bank managers who looked the part – early 50s, grey hair and dark suits – who were happy to work with us in a franchise arrangement because we were finding all the customers for them."

At its peak, more than 300 of these bankers across the country were working for Mark, and his central office with 100 staff occupied an entire business park near Norwich Airport.

Excess

Within a few months, Mark went from scraping money together to raise £10,000 to running a business that was rapidly growing and producing vast profits – and he finally had the means to emulate the property investors he'd spent the last seven years observing.

Having spent years diligently saving and planning for his first investment property, he was now in a position to scale his portfolio rapidly – but not to give it the same amount of research that he previously had.

"Only in hindsight can I attempt to justify it as some kind of strategy, but in reality I was just buying everything I could lay my hands on with very little thought: money was cheap and the market was booming. During the week I'd be arranging thousands of mortgages, and at the weekends my wife and I would drive around all the new showhomes going 'We'll have one of those, we'll have one of those'…it was a crazy, crazy time."

After so many lean years, Mark took the opportunity to let loose with his personal spending too. "At one point I had seven supercars at the same time. We were flying on holiday first class, having a house built in America…the proper playboy lifestyle. Imagine any rock star who finds sudden fame and goes totally off the rails – I was doing the mortgage broker version of that!"

By 2003, Mark had acquired "30 to 40" properties, worth a total of £4 million. He was too busy living the high life to buy any more, but still saw the value of his portfolio increase to £5 million by the end of the year. "Property prices went up 26% that year, and at the same time the amount lenders would give you went up from 75% to 85% of the property's value, so we were able to do a round of refinancing and put even more money in our bank account – all while we were basically on holiday. It was pure, pure luck."

Mark eventually toned down his lifestyle enough to find time to increase his property portfolio even more, and by 2008 he had bought 120 in total – some of which he flipped for a profit, and some he kept. As he'd long since passed the point where he could live off his rents and benefit from impressive capital growth, what kept him buying in such large numbers?

 "Ego. Pure ego about owning more property. I'd love to say that it was some phenomenal strategy, but although I've learnt a lot along the way, at the time it was just 'There's money in the bank – let's buy another property.' I loved being able to be the guy who would walk into a sales showroom, look around and say 'Yeah, we'll take four'!"

It wasn't just properties that Mark would buy on impulse. In 2004, a client offered to give Mark and his business partner a lift to the train station, and on the way they popped into a Bentley garage which was showcasing the latest model. Mark pulled out his new Coutts credit card at the end of the presentation and declared "I'll have one"; his business partner did the same and said "Make that two please!"

"I'd come from this working-class background, left school early, and had years of everyone saying 'all you can do is spin on your head.' This was my way of flicking everyone the bird and saying 'Look at me, I've got all these properties and I'm driving around in a Bentley.'"

But just a few years later the economy crashed, and Mark's fortunes changed dramatically.

Collapsing and regrouping

In 2008, Mark's business was turning over £28 million with a profit of £7 million. He was offered "between £17 and 20 million" to sell: an offer he and his business partners felt was too low, and refused.

Mere months later though, the global credit crunch meant that the securitised lending market almost completely dried up. His biggest lender, HBOS, merged with Lloyds – who decided they didn't want exposure to large brokers anymore, and terminated their contract immediately.

"The whole business model wasn't working anymore anyway, because it was all built around remortgaging when the value went up. Now though, values were dropping – so no more remortgaging, and no more business for us. It fell off a cliff almost literally overnight."

Less than a year after the offer to sell the company, Mark and his business partner made the painful decision to lay off every member of staff and put the business into hibernation.

At the same time, Mark was going through a divorce, and he found himself giving away a big chunk of money and property at the same time as losing his business. This focused his mind on how to manage his property portfolio more efficiently, and grow it in a more strategic way than he had done previously.

The solution he came up with was to stop operating on his own, and team up with members of his extended family. "I needed to consolidate my portfolio, and being emotionally low of course my thoughts turned towards my family at the same time. My parents and various other family members had got into property as a result of seeing my success, so we decided that we could do better by coming together rather than doing everything separately."

Their strategy was to buy at auction – pooling their resources to buy with cash – then either sell or refinance later. Whereas Mark's portfolio was within Norwich, his family was spread out all over the country, which allowed them to scour every auction for the best deals. "The properties we bought were largely concentrated around where the family lived – a lot in the Midlands, but we also had relatives in the North West. Somehow we ended up with one in Portsmouth, but I'm not sure how!"

"With 11 of us working together, we managed to look at hundreds of properties every month – say 30 that were in upcoming auctions, plus three comparables for each that were being sold on the open market. Then sometimes we'd buy none of them! At other auctions we'd buy half a dozen or more."

By buying with cash and researching each lot so diligently, the family was able to take full advantage of some of the astounding deals that were available as the economy slumped. "One example was the flat in Portsmouth, which had sold for £259,000 in 2003 and was being sold at auction in 2008 with a guide price of £65,000! We *knew* there was something wrong with it, but we couldn't work out what it was. In the end we bought it for £62,000, and the next day the company that was responsible for the management of the block went into liquidation. It took us over two years to track down all the other leaseholders and buy the management rights back, but doing it solved the problem and the flat was worth £250,000 again. The property was unfinanceable that entire time, so you can only do that kind of deal if you can buy with cash and have the flexibility to hold it for as long as necessary."

Management

Another advantage of working with his family was that Mark could delegate the maintenance of his properties to his brother: a builder and project manager. Until that point, management had taken a distant second place to acquisition in Mark's list of priorities.

"We tried self-managing for a while when we were first building the portfolio, and ballsed it up totally. Money didn't really matter, so we spent a fortune fixing things and sometimes didn't even bother reletting properties as they became empty because we were too busy flying off on holiday."

"If we hadn't been making so much money from the capital appreciation and the business, we would have gone bust through our own stupidity. Eventually we noticed that our bank balance was going down instead of up because we were wasting so much money, so we had to do something about it."

A temporary solution came in the form of one of Mark's tenants: an HR manager at a big mobile phone repair factory who referred newly arrived Polish and Lithuanian workers to Mark's properties and took care of the management in return for living rent-free.

Bringing the management fully into the family, though, allowed Mark to turn it into one of the core strengths of his property business – rather than the necessary evil it had previously been.

"We've issued over a thousand tenancies, and only had to go to court twice to seek possession. Maybe it's luck, but I like to think it's because we've got systems in place and we apply common sense to our referencing and letting processes."

To start with, Mark almost doubles his pool of potential tenants by omitting one of the most common phrases in property adverts: "No pets".

"Instead, we say 'Pets considered – guarantors may be required.' Because would you really object to someone keeping a goldfish if they were a good tenant? I like to visit potential tenants in their homes anyway to see how they live, so I can meet their pets at the same time. If it's a massive Rottweiler and there are claw marks over all the furniture then maybe not, but considering pets is the easiest way to increase the number of tenants who'll be interested in your property."

Mark wants his tenants to stay as long as possible to minimise voids, and has started demonstrating this using a document called a Deed of Assurance. The Deed states that if the tenants have done nothing wrong and Mark asks them to leave within five years, he'll pay them money to compensate them. This gives good tenants peace of mind, while still allowing Mark to legally evict them if they don't pay their rent.

"It's playing with their psychology, really. The amazing thing is that tenants who *don't* want to stay for a long time won't sign a Deed of Assurance – even though it's only me that's being tied in, not them! They just hear 'five years', don't listen properly and go and look elsewhere. People who *do* want to stay for five years will listen intently, understand it and love it."

Financing

An unusual element of Mark's investing strategy is his practice of taking on maximum leverage, but keeping an amount equivalent to 20% of his total borrowings as cash in his bank account. For example, if he had mortgages totalling £5 million, he would keep £1 million as cash in the bank.

In most cases someone would only borrow the amount they needed, and hope to see their loan-to-value percentage fall over time as property prices go up. Mark, though, would use the opportunity to borrow more to take him back up to the maximum – but leave a healthy amount of it in the bank.

"Let's take a simple example from when I was a mortgage broker. Someone would come to me and say they wanted to buy a house for £100,000 and borrow £60,000 to do it. I'd say fine, that'll cost you £250 a month in repayments, or whatever it would be. But why not pay an extra £100 or so a month, then you can borrow an extra £25,000 and keep it in the bank?"

"They'd say 'Oh no, I don't feel safe borrowing the maximum.' But my argument would be: if the apocalypse happens, property prices halve, interest rates double and all your boilers break down at once…would you rather have been saving £100 each month, or have £25,000 in the bank?"

Mark is at pains to point out that his figure of 20% cash reserves isn't an arbitrary number. When he was working with businesses in the early 1990s and two-thirds of them were going bust, it was the ones with cash in the bank that survived – and when he studied the patterns, 20% was the cut-off point that demarcated the ones that went under from the ones who thrived.

"I didn't invent this rule, I just spotted it. Maybe I was the first person to spot the trend and put a badge on it, or maybe it was only a trend among the people I worked with. But it's worked out well for me."

Most people would worry that the costs of the extra borrowing would put a dent in their monthly cashflow and expose them to more risk when interest rates go up, but Mark isn't concerned. "At some point in the next ten years, the base rate will be 6–7% – but I'll still be cashflow positive. And whatever happens, holding the cash in the bank is costing me very little because if interest rates go up, the rate I'll get in a savings account will go up too."

"And anyway, if interest rates go up suddenly it'll be because something seriously positive has happened in the economy, and I'll take advantage of that. No one else will be able to, because they've got all their money tied up in their property!"

Buying bungalows

These days, Mark feels like he has enough properties – "They're making me good money, so why add to my headaches by buying more?" – but he can't resist joining with his family in buying properties to sell straight on for a profit.

At the moment, they're mostly buying bungalows: "Old ones where someone's died, it's not been refurbed since the 1960s and it's sitting on a big plot of land. Worst house, good street, lots of land – simple as that. We're adding value by gutting them and extending them – taking the roof off and putting 40–60% extra onto the floor area. You need full planning permission and it's a lot of work, but we can get a 40% return on our capital within six months without having to buy at a particularly great price or anything like that."

Mark feels that working with his family overcomes what he perceives as his main weakness: losing attention. "If something doesn't capture me, even if it's important, I'll just wander off. So if I need to make sure I've got people around me who'll be there to sort things out if my attention drifts. My business partner always used to say that I was driving a lorry down the motorway at 100 miles per hour, cargo spilling everywhere, and he was running behind me putting all the boxes back on."

At the same time, if something *does* capture Mark, "I'm infatuated, and I'll go into more and more detail forever until I know everything." What captures him most is human behaviour: "I'm obsessed with following the habits of successful people and deconstructing what works. Who should I be copying when it comes to their tax strategy? Or their borrowing profile? Everything starts with human behaviour. Like, why do people rent certain properties? Understanding that will help mine rent faster if there's a lot of competition."

What now?

Mark is now facing a decision that few people have at age 45: his children have grown up, he's happily remarried, he's financially independent and doesn't need to be personally involved with his investments…what next?

For now he's happy doing what he's always done: filling his week days with emails and phone calls, and spending his weekends meeting up with the family to do viewings and discuss deals. "I love the problem-solving aspect, I like being in a position to help people, and I like the prestige that comes with it. I like the money too, but if I could do it for nothing and still have the problem-solving and the prestige, I would. I suppose I could just play Monopoly all day, but it's not quite the same."

When it comes to how he could spend his money, Mark feels like he's done it all already. "It sounds sad, but I did everything I dreamed of doing and couldn't think of anything else to do other than do some of them again. I've had the playboy lifestyle and there's no need to go back to that."

"I actually like the idea of just travelling around in a nice caravan, although my wife would need some persuading. If I could win her over, I could just leave my portfolio being managed and go do that for a while."

"Then one day I might just say sod it, I'll pay the capital gains tax and sell the lot – I'm off."

Lessons

Borrow your eggs and put them in multiple baskets

"People will often say to me that they don't like risk, and they'd prefer to get all their income from one property with no mortgage on it – but that would scare me to death! Firstly, fear of loss: if your tenant stops paying you've lost 100% of your income, whereas if I had four properties with mortgages I'd only lose 25% if one of my tenants didn't pay. Secondly, missed opportunities to gain: if property prices double, I could have had four properties doubling in value rather than just one."

Cash reserves are the best protection against whatever happens

"A lot of people think my strategy of keeping 20% in liquid funds is crazy, but in all the businesses I've analysed, that's the figure that separates success from failure when things hit the fan. Of course it's tempting to spend those reserves when there are good deals on the table: it's a principle as opposed to a rule, and I've failed miserably to stick to it on many occasions."

There's no point in worrying pre-emptively

"A lot people worry about things that are never going to happen: 'What am I going to do when I've got all these properties to look after? All these mortgage applications to keep on top of?' Well, worry about it when it happens, because by then you'll have the money and knowledge to sort it out!"

There's big money in bungalows

"Developers don't like building bungalows because they can't fit as many onto a given plot of land, yet at the same time there are baby boomers reaching retirement and wanting to downsize. High demand and low supply is always a recipe for making money."

"The baby boomers want something nice to move into, yet the bungalows on the market are normally tired. The owners or beneficiaries just want to get shot of them though, to get their money out. That makes for a great development opportunity for investors with good refurbishment skills or a trusted team of tradesmen."

Jonathan Clarke

"The credit crunch was the best thing since sliced bread!"

Jonathan parks his people carrier by the ex-council development in Milton Keynes where he's visiting a tenant, and he shuts the door gingerly. The wing mirror – which is taped in place – is constantly on the brink of falling off. The central locking has been broken for months, so he makes a big pantomime of pretending to lock the doors. In his scruffs, fingerless gloves and resolutely non-swish car, Jonathan is often mistaken as the builder of a property rather than the buyer.

If someone said "property investor" to you, Jonathan's is not the image that would come to mind. But in fact, he's the archetypal "millionaire next door": he's in his early 50s, recently retired from the police, and has earned financial freedom from a decade of highly successful buy-to-let investments.

The surprising thing is that rather than pay someone £20,000 a year to look after his portfolio so he can spend his days on a beach somewhere, Jonathan far prefers to manage his 45 properties himself. He rarely leaves Milton Keynes, never has a day off, and is happiest when he's sitting in his dressing gown going through the post with the cricket on in the background.

That's because property is Jonathan's hobby. He describes his tenants as "as close to friends as tenants can be", and is known on online property forums for his thoughtful, philosophical posts about investment and life in general. Although Jonathan's idea of an endgame is different from many other people's, the fulfilment he's found in his investing life is something that anyone would aspire to.

Walking the beat

Jonathan enjoyed a solidly middle-class upbringing in Oxfordshire, where his father – a banker with Barclays – instilled in him an appreciation of sensible saving from an early age. "From as soon as I got my first Coventry Building Society book, I enjoyed seeing the interest being added. My dad invested in shares, and he talked a lot about the importance of putting your money away – because you don't want to be working all your life and you'll need money at the end of the game, as it were."

He flunked his A-levels ("I was more interested in wine, women and song") and went to work as a paste-up artist for Robert Maxwell. "There were 20 of us in an open-plan office, joking around all day – it was just like school!" After three years though, the introduction of computers made his job obsolete, and he realised it was time to move on.

Jonathan saw an advert in the *Oxford Times* recruiting for the police service – "There were pictures of someone chasing a baddie, helping an old lady across the road...I thought, 'I could do that!'" – and despite reservations from his mother, he joined. He spent his first couple of years in the force stationed in Windsor, before being transferred to Milton Keynes in 1983.

At the time he was being paid £8,000 a year, and on arriving in Milton Keynes he realised that property prices were so much cheaper than in Windsor that he could afford to buy his own house. "I was completely naive about the buying process – I remember the estate agent showing me around eight properties and me asking him, 'Well, which one do you think I should buy?' I'm sure he sold me a dog of a property at full price, but I was just happy at age 23 to have my own home."

The home was a three-bed semi in Bletchley where he lived alone for six months, until his girlfriend Gina (the sister of his best friend from school) moved in. She was a maths teacher, and every day she'd ride the ten miles to her school on a 125cc Suzuki motorcycle ("called Oscar"). Some of the roads were dark and treacherous in the winter, so they started looking for a new home closer to where she worked.

They found a one-bedroom flat to the north of Milton Keynes, which they could afford in addition to keeping his existing house. They completed for £17,000, buying it in Gina's name, and leaving his place sitting empty. "How mad is that! I was interested in property just because prices were on the up, and it didn't occur to me to make the most of the investment by doing something as obvious as putting a tenant in."

When Jonathan and Gina married in 1986, they decided that they'd like to move to a new house in Stony Stratford. They needed to sell his empty house to fund the purchase, but Jonathan wanted to keep hold of their current flat. Gina wasn't keen, so they sold it and pocketed a £9,000 profit. The money came in very useful at the time, but still irks Jonathan to see that it's now worth £110,000. "I always think back to that flat when I'm tempted to sell a property now."

They moved several more times as their three daughters were born, and Jonathan concentrated on his job in the police – moving into the relatively new field of restorative justice, which he loved. But the desire to do something with property was lying dormant in him – and a disastrous episode in 1999 brought it back to the surface.

A winning formula

Aged 40, sixteen years after buying his first house, Jonathan slipped a disc and spent three months lying flat on his back in the living room of the house where he still lives today.

"I was bored. Bored bored bored bored! While lying there, I thought about what would happen if I had to leave the police. My wife left work in 1988 to look after our first daughter, and with the birth of our other two daughters she didn't start back part-time until 1997. We didn't feel able to contribute to her teacher's pension during that whole time. We had about £150,000 of equity in our own home at the time, so I told Gina that if we used it to buy another house, that could be her pension." She was naturally very risk-averse, but she agreed.

They increased their mortgage by £44,000 and bought a house with cash. Jonathan wasn't thinking about cashflow or buying it at a good price – just that "I knew property prices were going up, and in 30 years this would make a good pension." They put a tenant in, made £100 a month after their costs, and Jonathan became more convinced than ever that property was the answer.

Over the next year Jonathan saw the value of his first buy-to-let going up and up, and he wanted to buy more. First though, he had a major obstacle to overcome: convincing Gina that it was a good idea.

Using all the negotiation skills he'd learnt in his day job, Jonathan appealed to her interests. "My wife loves two things: charity shops, and her children. So first, I gave her £20 from our rental profits to go to a charity shop. That went down well!"

"Then I said to her, 'Look, I've got my police pension and you've now got a property as a pension, but what about our three poor children?'"

The tactic worked, so in 2000 he took out a mortgage on the now-increased value of their first investment property. Using those funds, he subsequently took out three 85% buy-to-let mortgages to buy three more houses.

All of his thoughts until that point had been solely about capital growth (although he was at least now remembering to put tenants in place), but two of his new properties were bought more with cashflow in mind. They were flats in unfashionable parts of town, which were cheap to buy but brought in roughly the same amount of rent as those in nicer areas. This type of property makes up the bulk of his portfolio today.

"It was a nice strong period of capital growth so I'd be buying for £25,000; by the time I completed they'd be worth £30,000, and a few months later they'd be worth £33,000. So on paper I'd made £8,000 in about six months, and only put in about £3,500 in cash because I was using 85% mortgages. So, naturally, I really went for it!"

Having found his winning formula, Jonathan bought another three or four properties each year for the next ten years. He bought, "stuck tenants in willy-nilly, and paid the price on some of them", and moved on to the next one.

Jonathan now has around 45 properties and says he's stopped buying – for now, at least – but unlike so many other investors it wasn't the credit crunch that stopped him. "The credit crunch was the best thing since sliced bread! I was getting letters through the door telling me my mortgage repayments had gone down by £40, £60 a month. It made me think a bit about my business and what could go wrong, but if this is a recession I'm having a bloody good one!"

In fact, Jonathan only stopped buying in 2012 when he was turned down for finance by the lender he's used for most of his properties, The Mortgage Works. "I was furious at the time, but after 24 hours I'd calmed down and realised it was a nice excuse to keep my cash and not have to do any more. I can't promise to have stopped forever, but I'm enjoying it for now."

Case study

Four-bedroom house in Haywards Croft, Milton Keynes MK12

Upfront expenses:

Purchase price: £100,000 in 2012

Refurb costs: £3,000

Legal and purchase fees: £1,000

Gross monthly rental income: £1,000 (£950 LHA rate plus £50 top-up from the tenant)

Monthly expenses:

Mortgage: £355 (75% LTV at 5.49% fixed for five years)

£50 allowance for maintenance

£10 insurance

Net monthly profit: £585

Return on cash invested: Approximately 25%

This purchase is close to the prototypical deal that Jonathan looks for: a three or four-bedroom house that's "a bit beaten up: not wrecked enough to attract a developer or trader, but a bit too much wrong with it to attract a novice developer".

The property needed £3,000 of works to make it habitable, and Jonathan will finish off the works in 2017 – just before the five-year fixed rate mortgage expires. "In 2017 – with a full refurb and another few years of capital growth – it might be worth £140,000, so I could remortgage at 75% loan-to-value for £105,000."

"The monthly mortgage payment at a 5% interest rate would be £437, so it would still be making me a net profit of around £500, and I would have pulled all my original cash back out except for the refurb costs. I could then take that cash, buy another property and repeat the exercise. I'm supposed to have stopped buying, of course, but we'll see if that lasts!"

Jonathan has never concerned himself too much with buying below market value, because most of his purchases were at a time when values were steadily increasing anyway. "I normally just buy 5–10% below if I can, and move on to the next one...if I'd spent a year looking for the perfect 20% BMV deal, I'd have missed out on £3,600 in the meantime."

"With this particular property, the interesting thing is that a couple of weeks into the buying process an identical house came up for auction with a guide price of £75,000. At the time it looked like I'd just paid £25,000 over the odds, but in the end I was pleased to see that it sold at auction for £101,000. That showed me that I'd paid the right price for mine."

Two key ingredients

At first glance, it might look like Jonathan has just been lucky. After all, he's benefited from a period of capital growth that new investors can never dream of seeing again.

But many other investors – with exactly the same market conditions – either didn't capitalise on them, or went too far and ended up with piles of debt and no cashflow. Jonathan's sensible, patient approach certainly helped, but his success seems to hang mainly on his embracing of two things that many others shy away from: debt, and what he describes as the "hardcore LHA" market.

"I was never fearful of the LHA market, because many of my tenants were the people I interacted with in my police job. Sure, sometimes there's litter everywhere, and drug needles, and loud music, and they call you up at all hours...but that's just like at work!"

"At the time I thought everyone dealt with these characters: I didn't know any other property investors, so I had no idea that other people would run a mile from the kind of thing I was doing."

Not only does Jonathan personally manage all 45 of his properties, but he actively enjoys it. "I like interesting people who bring stories of their lives into my life. I like the sociability of popping in and having a cup of tea with my tenants."

He describes his management style as "soft, but with a hard business brain behind it. I don't chase up the odd £20 I'm owed here and there, so hopefully they think 'Oh, he's a good old boy' and I get referrals because of it. I used to get wound up and think 'You owe me £10 from five years ago!' every time I saw someone, but I learnt to let it go. I lose a lot of money, but I make a lot more."

"A lot of these people are desperate, they're on the breadline, and I'm always conscious of that. It keeps your feet on the ground."

A collaborative approach

Jonathan has a collaborative approach in all aspects of his business, and never more so than with his tenants – with whom he puts together flexible arrangements that create "a good deal for them, and a better deal for me".

"When I buy a new property, I aim to get access before completion to make it habitable, then find a tenant to move in on the same day – cutting down voids to the bare bones. I'll try to find a tenant who has a positive attitude towards doing the place up in return for a roof over their head. Many of them have come to me from a hostel, their mate's sofa, their car, the street...it might look like a wreck to you and me but to them it's a palace, and it represents freedom and a fresh start."

Because his tenants are collaborators in their own home, they tend to stay a long time and do a lot of the maintenance themselves. "I just had a guy leave me after five years: I had £300 of maintenance costs during that period, and visited him once a year." Now he has a large portfolio, he'll move tenants to larger or smaller houses as their circumstances change – "I had a five-house chain once!"

These "can-do" tenants often have friends who can do refurbishment work, with Jonathan just paying for materials – and even then he's had whole kitchens, bathrooms, radiators and carpets for free. For maintenance that has to be done by someone else, he calls on his network of "eccentric but experienced, slightly 'past their sell-by date' one-man-band types, and keen up-and-coming lads who'll turn out at midnight but don't know what a call-out charge is".

This "symbiotic" approach obviously depends on finding the right type of tenant in the first place, and Jonathan has a homebrew approach to that process as well: rather than any kind of formal referencing, he just spends a couple of hours talking to people who apply. Often he'll know them anyway because they're a friend or relative of an existing tenant.

"I used to fling people into properties quickly just to move on to the next one, but now I'm a lot more thorough: if someone's going to be with me for five years or more, two hours at the start is neither here nor there. I've never done a credit check in my life – I like to think that from my job I've developed the skills to size people up face-to-face."

"I spend a couple of hours digging into their mental attitude towards debt, their mental attitude towards looking after a place, and them as a person: can I trust that even if they get into trouble, they'll pay me back? I try to see them in their current home if possible, because it's hard to hide your lifestyle."

Beating bureaucracy

The other side of the LHA equation, of course, is the council. Here too, Jonathan's experience from his multi-agency role in the police has helped him develop a pragmatic attitude towards dealing with bureaucracy.

"I used to get angry at the council because they weren't being professional – I was acting professionally, so why couldn't they? But now I treat the council just like another tenant – a tenant who sometimes pays and sometimes doesn't. There's no point throwing my toys out of the pram, because then I'll just go to the bottom of their pile."

"They're understaffed and underpaid, so if they don't reply to an email within 24 hours it's not because they're being malicious – they just can't do it. They have a ten-day turnaround, that's just how it works, so if it goes over ten days I'll send a gentle reminder."

Jonathan currently has arrangements with the council to be paid directly for most of his tenants, but with Universal Credit coming in, he'll have to adapt his systems to being paid by the tenant for all new claims.

"I don't want Universal Credit to happen – it's a bit of a headache – but I'm sure we'll get round it. I plan to use the MK Credit Union. I've had the situation before where the majority of it was paid to the tenants so I know what it's like and it's not enough to make me throw in the towel, but I can see why other people would stay away from LHA as a result."

"In a way it might be a good thing because it turns the power tables with the council – I always feel at their mercy, but if other landlords start giving up on LHA, I'll be in a position of power because they won't want me to do the same."

Happily indebted

As well as his embracing of the LHA market, the other defining characteristic of Jonathan's success has been his willingness to take on large amounts of debt to magnify his returns – he estimates that he has £5 million worth of mortgages in total.

While the credit crunch caused lots of people to reconsider their levels of debt and shift their focus towards paying it down, Jonathan still has no interest in reducing his leverage. "A buy-and-hold strategy works because it produces cashflow – so I can't see why you'd want to reverse that strategy. I think the reason people pay off debt is that there's a nagging feeling that it's somehow reckless or irresponsible or greedy to have hundreds of thousands of debt. My generation was brought up with the 'pay off your mortgage as soon as you can' attitude, and I have to battle against the wind sometimes to demonstrate why I don't."

"My 87-year-old mother has paid off her mortgage – that makes her feel comfortable. I'd prefer to take out the equity, buy 20 houses with it and dwarf her pension with the cashflow, but that just goes against the grain for her."

"In total, I've got just shy of £5 million of debt. It doesn't faze me at all. I remember someone saying once that if you've got £10,000 of debt that's your problem, but if you've got £10 million in debt that's the bank's problem! I'll never get down to zero debt, so there's no point pretending I will. I'll just let the 10/15/20 years run on the mortgages, and maybe sell some when they become due."

He also doesn't worry too much about keeping large cash reserves. "Not all the boilers are going to go at the same time, so I don't feel like I need too much in the bank. And anyway, if it came to it, I could raise £100,000 in a few months pretty easily – there are always personal loans and credit cards. Or shock horror, I might actually have to sell one! I can see how other people could see it as sailing too close to the wind, though."

Switching down a gear

Jonathan cut back to a three-day week in 2005 – six years after he had started investing – because his rental income had started to exceed his full-time salary at work.

He then fully retired in October 2011, but says that his life now isn't too different from the last 30 years of his working life – because he's always enjoyed what he does, and has always managed to carve out roles where he's his own boss. His full-time job is now managing his portfolio, but "full-time" doesn't seem like quite the right description.

"I'm a potterer. I potter. I get up at 6am and the rest of the family doesn't rise until a couple of hours later, so I'll have a cup of tea, put on Sky News, and read the paper if I didn't read it the day before. I've got my clipboard of things to do that day, with asterisks by the ones that I *must* do. Those 'got to do' jobs take maybe an hour or two – going to see someone, or making a couple of phone calls."

"Other than that I'll just slob around in my dressing gown all day – tidying up a bit here, watching a bit of telly there, going on the computer...I love the freedom of it. I like sitting in my chair, seeing people go past on their way to work, and thinking 'Yeah...I've worked hard, and now I don't have to do that anymore.' Each day is a pure luxury."

Even though he can now do pretty much as he pleases, personally managing his properties means that Jonathan can never really go away or shift his focus to something else – and he's fine with that. "I don't particularly like travelling and holidays, I don't like beaches, I like cars but I don't like new cars...if I had some time away from my business, I'd probably start another business! "

"Look at people like Bruce Forsyth who are still going in their 80s...they don't need to do that, but they love it. I'm the same: property is my hobby. There must be something else I want to do, but I've not made the time to find it. Sometimes I do feel like I've neglected other areas of my life by being so wrapped up in my hobby, but I've been at every one of my kids' sports days, and I get all the sociability I need from my tenants, my family and a few mates.

The fact that property is more of a hobby than a job is borne out by Jonathan's contributions to online forums, where he's known and respected for his contemplative posts in a medium that tends to attract more argumentative and competitive interactions.

"Until I went online I had no idea there were all these other property people in the world! It's almost like internet dating: I'll meet someone from the forums and feel like I already know them well because we've got property in common. They might be from the other end of the country, but I like knowing that if I'm ever passing through Wales or Eastbourne there's someone I can pop in on. These people online are almost like my "colleagues" now that I've left the police – they've met the need for sociability that I used to get at work."

The future

When Jonathan considers the future, he knows that he'll have to pass the management over to someone else at some point. "I want a mirror image of myself who sees exactly how I want things done, but just needs a bit of guidance in how to do it. That probably means employing and training someone directly rather than using an agent."

"I'm not in any rush though: as it is I can just sit around in my dressing gown and occasionally toddle off to do something. If I passed over the management I'd have *nothing* to do every morning, and then I'd have to face up to what to do next."

Jonathan is also scratching his property-buying itch by finding and managing properties for other investors. "I get to live vicariously through them, view lots of properties and earn some pocket money in return for doing what I love."

When it comes to his own portfolio, his thoughts are turning towards succession planning as his daughters are now 25, 23 and 20. "I've got to work out how to pass things on in the most tax-efficient way...I don't know how to do it in detail yet, but I'll learn."

In fact, it seems likely that his next venture will be determined by his daughters in one way or another. "One of my daughters is very much into animals, and if she said she wanted to start a business around that I'd happily get involved. We could open up an educational facility where children come on school trips to learn about animals. It would make money, and I'd get to see the excitement on the kids' faces every morning...that sounds pretty good to me."

Lessons

Reality is what you make it

The old cliché that "if you love what you do, you'll never work a day in your life" is certainly true for Jonathan. He has the same interactions with tenants, solicitors and agents as any other investor, but because he's inclined to put a positive spin on things he gets far more enjoyment out of identical experiences.

Work as a team with your tenants and tradesmen

Jonathan's job in the police obviously helped him to develop a consultative approach, but because he genuinely likes people it comes naturally. It makes for happier relationships, saves him money, and makes his business run more smoothly.

Debt doesn't have to be bad

As many people discovered in the credit crunch, there are levels of debt that are unambiguously too high. But as long as debt is used within sensible boundaries as a deliberate part of a plan, there's no need to feel pressure to pay it down.

You can factor in problems from the start

"Over a 30-year investing career, property prices will go down at some point, interest rates will go up, mortgage deals will dry up. These things are a given, so stress-test your portfolio and plan for them from the start."

Done right, property isn't risky

"People need property to live in. England is relatively small and crowded. Your property will rent out. They're not building nearly enough housing to meet demand. If treated with respect, property is indeed as safe as houses."

Property is a psychologically attractive investment

"People buy their own houses and turn them into a home. They'd do it even if prices were controlled by the government and it was illegal to make any money from it. As an investor you can do that, *and* have the lovely feeling that you're making money from it. That's dynamite."

Just get started

"A journey of a thousand miles starts with a single step. Get educated, get your mindset sorted, and be fearless but not foolish. Buy in good times and in bad, and don't give up."

Nichola Baker

"I know I'll pay them back, and they must believe me."

"My friends call me The Socialist Capitalist," Nichola laughs. "They can't understand how a social worker would end up owning nine properties, and everyone at work thought I was nuts."

"Then again, one of my colleagues invested £10,000 with me, so I must have given *some* impression that I know what I was doing…"

Native Kiwi Nichola has made astonishingly fast progress in property: she only bought her own home in 2006, her first investment properties in 2009, and didn't quit her job until 2013. But if that implies an easy ride, it wasn't: there were years of driving a 500-mile round trip to manage her properties and, in 2011, one bad decision meant she almost lost everything.

"I think the negative is a better motivation than the positive, and adversity keeps me moving forward. But the positive motivation has always been the dream of being able to go back to New Zealand without having to worry about money…and now my flights are booked, and later this year it's actually going to happen."

Escaping the edge of the earth

Nichola moved to England in August 2001, aged 27. "It felt like New Zealand was on the edge of the earth, and that's not what you want when you're 27. I had just qualified as a social worker, and I moved as much for the job opportunities as anything. I was offered three jobs almost as soon as I arrived."

Even though social work was a vocation, she only ever planned to do it for ten years: she knew that she needed to earn money that she could invest in assets that would give her freedom, so why not earn that money by helping people?

"For some reason I'd always had this idea that I'd be wealthy and free by age 45, but I had no idea how that would happen. I was addicted to self-development books, and had a journal full of all the notes I'd written, so I knew from those books that being an employee wasn't the answer. But of course, I needed to earn money."

Nichola also had a strong desire to own her own house. She wasn't thinking about property as her route to becoming wealthy by age 45, but just wanted the security of having somewhere of her own.

Before she could even think about buying a house though, she had to clear £12,000 of student debt and save up a deposit. "For years I took the smallest room in shared houses, and I was no stranger to two-minute noodles."

Comings and goings

Five years later, her frugality had paid off: her debts had been cleared, and she had £20,000 in her bank account to use as a deposit.

Her circumstances had also changed in other ways: she married a fellow Antipodean in 2005, and quickly became pregnant. Needing stability and no longer able to live in shared houses, in June 2006 she and her husband bought a house in Brockley, South East London, for their new family to live in. It needed a large-scale refurb ("We were ripping the place apart, dust everywhere, while my son was a few weeks old"), but it was hers.

Unfortunately though, her marriage was "dicey", and by September 2007 they'd separated. Nichola and her son went back to New Zealand for a few months to be with her parents, returning in March 2008 to start afresh. She bought her husband out of his share of the house, and started a new social work contract in Southwark.

"By this point I was laden with debt from buying my ex-husband out. My mortgage was £900 a month, and I was spending £800 a month on childcare so I could go and work at this awful council job that I hated. I remember sitting on the bus back home thinking, 'There must be more to life than this.'"

A special delivery

In May 2008, just as she was at her lowest ebb, Nichola noticed a leaflet through her door from Women in Wealth – a training organisation to help women take control of their financial future, with an emphasis on property investment. "Looking back, if ever there was a sign that things are meant to be, that was it."

"I went along to the free session they'd been advertising and sat at the back with my arms folded, but I was won over and ended up signing up to a three-day course on the spot."

It was the start of a property education programme that saw Nichola loading up her already stretched credit cards with £11,000 for three courses and a three-day mentorship. Although she was aware of the reputation of many property courses even then, she was desperate to take action – "I knew I could do it, but I needed someone holding my hand and keeping me on track."

The courses covered distressed property, buy-to-let, and lease options – and the quality of the content was "mixed". "Learning about lease options was like a lightbulb going off, but I wasn't about to run out and start doing it. I felt like I needed to be a landlord first, so that I'd have the confidence to go into a vendor's home and start talking about all this stuff."

Discovering Barrow

As part of her training, Nichola had paid for three days "on location" with a mentor, and she was asked to decide which location to focus on.

"I'd spent a lot of money so I was determined to pick the right area and not waste the opportunity. I knew it couldn't be London because of the high rents and low yields, but I couldn't just go anywhere because I had my son to look after. So I looked in Chatham, Maidstone and all around Kent, but I just couldn't make the numbers work. The rental wasn't high enough to support the values."

In the midst of her disillusionment about finding a suitable area near London, Nichola realised that a good friend of hers had moved to Kendal in Cumbria. It was a five-hour drive away, but her friend would happily look after her son for free – giving Nichola a whole new area to explore.

"On a map, I drew a circle to show where I could get to within an hour's drive of Kendal. I looked at places like Bradford and Keighley and realised that almost everywhere, the yields were so much better than in London. The place that really jumped out at me was Barrow-in-Furness – the yields seemed to be about 12% for a single let, and I'd read about a big 12-year regeneration project for the town's marina."

So she set a date for her mentorship ("I'm pretty sure he had to look it up when I said 'Barrow'"), left her son in Kendal, and arrived in Barrow for the first time. "I was terrified that he'd say I was wasting his time, and what on earth was I doing dragging him all the way up here. But he said it reminded him of Hull, where he invested, with the added advantage of less competition from other investors. That made me feel better."

They spent the weekend viewing at least 30 properties, and putting in "embarrassingly low offers. None of them got accepted, but it didn't matter. I was learning, and I felt more strongly than ever that I could do this."

Becoming a landlord

Back in London and back at work, Nichola was more certain than ever that she wanted to get into property. Although she'd found a promising area to invest in, she didn't have the time to source properties in another part of the country, so she found a sourcing company online and signed up to see what they had available.

The first deal that came up was in Liverpool, and the following weekend she drove up to see it. "It was a total mess. The vendor was desperate to sell, and said she'd even throw in the white goods. I thought, well, at least that's one thing to cross off the list. I got about 50 metres down the road, pulled over, and called the company to say I'd take it."

At the same time she viewed properties in Carlisle and Barrow, and decided to buy those too – although she was £10,000 short of the legal and refurbishment funds she needed to buy the Carlisle property. Not willing to let the deal slip, she called the vendor and arranged to take the £10,000 as a loan, repayable in 18 months – a technique known as "vendor financing", which she had learnt from her courses and would come to use again in the future. "The vendor was getting divorced and couldn't afford to stay, so she was just happy to get out and didn't need all the money immediately."

The transactions went through slowly, and all three ended up completing in the same week – the start of February 2009 – while Nichola was back in New Zealand visiting her family. "I very deliberately bought three at once to get into the mindset of 'Bang bang bang, this is how you do it.' I wanted it to become second nature, because at the time it wasn't second nature at all. I think I drove everyone in the process nuts because I was asking a thousand questions about how they did what they did…I just wanted to learn."

The three properties generated a profit of £800 a month, and word of Nichola's burgeoning empire started to spread. A work colleague had £10,000 sitting in the bank and wanted to put it to better use, so Nichola pooled it with her own savings to buy a small three-bedroom house in Barrow at auction for £49,000. "I could probably buy something similar for £35,000 knowing what I do now, but you learn as you go along. I gave my investor 20% interest on her investment – far more than I'd ever give away now – but I wanted to build my reputation and encourage other people to invest in me."

Suddenly, in a very short space of time, Nichola had become a landlord with four properties under her belt. She was still working extra shifts, looking after her son and spending her weekends on property, but she was on her way.

Getting creative

Now that Nichola had two properties in Barrow, she started putting cards through the doors of all the houses nearby to drum up leads to acquire more. It didn't take long before someone called – "he owned number 19, and I owned number 5, on the same street".

It was a big six-bedroom house, and Nichola knew that big properties in the area were scarce and in high demand. "I was very keen and trying not to show it…bluffing all the way!"

The vendor wanted to get out, but Nichola didn't have the funds. "He'd bought it four years earlier, but then his marriage broke up and he was never able to do what he intended to do with the property. From talking to him I knew that he didn't need the money until he was getting married again in six months' time, so we agreed that I'd buy it now, he'd effectively loan me the money, and I'd pay him back in six months." Determined not to get into any more debt to make the purchase, "I tightened my belt, took on even more shifts, and paid him his money on time."

Just as she'd done in Carlisle, Nichola had used vendor financing to do a deal that wouldn't otherwise have been possible. "I'd never use it with a vendor who's in serious distress, but in the right circumstances it means I can do deals that are in everyone's best interests. It's problem solving. With the Barrow one in particular I didn't negotiate as hard as I would do now, but I'd still never do a deal where anyone felt like they were being fleeced."

The surprising thing is that she's never put contracts in place for the money she's effectively borrowed from the vendor. "If I was in their position, by heck I'd have a charge on the property! But they don't think of it – I know I'll pay them back, and they must believe me. That must be a testament to the relationship I build with them."

Delayed gratification

The investor who sold her the big house in Barrow clearly didn't feel fleeced: he passed on Nichola's card to a lady he knew was trying to sell her house – giving Nichola another opportunity to find a creative solution.

The vendor had knocked two houses together to make one big house with a ground-floor bedroom and bathroom, to suit her son who had MS. "But her son died, then a few months later her partner died of a heart attack. It was just a tragic, awful situation – she was desperate to move because of all the memories the house contained."

Nichola couldn't afford to put down a deposit to get a mortgage, so her solution was to find a tenant buyer: someone who wanted to buy the house eventually but needed time before they could get a mortgage. The tenant buyer would put down a small amount upfront to subsidise the deposit Nichola needed for her mortgage, then pay rent until they were ready to get a mortgage themselves and buy it from Nichola. Their rent would include a "top up" each month, which would be taken off the eventual purchase price.

"I just couldn't find the right person, and this went on for five months – the whole time having the vendor calling me crying and begging me to buy it. Eventually, I found a couple in the next street who really wanted the house because the wife had a degenerative illness and needed the disabled access. They had 21 grandchildren, so a big house for when they visited plus a ground-floor bedroom for them was perfect."

They weren't interested in buying the house because they were too old to get a mortgage, so they agreed to lend Nichola the money she needed for a deposit, interest-free for three years, in return for an agreement that they could rent the property securely until one of them died. The rent was enough to cover Nichola's mortgage and not much more, but she was happy just to have found a solution and have the prospect of long-term capital growth.

"I probably bought it with my heart rather than my head, and I didn't see any money for years. But as it happens, after three years the couple moved out into a smaller place, so I turned the property into an HMO which now generates £1,000 profit. The couple who moved out are reinvesting their money with me, with interest this time, enabling the husband to give up his job and become my property manager and handyman. They even babysit my son sometimes!"

"I'm a firm believer that if you help people, the rewards will come eventually. I bought a property that made me no money, but helped two sets of people – and I ended up with a handyman, a babysitter, a lifelong friendship and *eventually* the chance to make a profit from it. I think being a social worker has made me able to spot opportunities to help people, and if you do that the rewards can't help coming eventually."

Managing from a distance

While Nichola was building up her portfolio in Barrow, she was still working in London – so throughout 2009 she drove up every two weeks to have meetings and do what needed to be done.

"My son's father would have him every other weekend, so I'd drop him off on Friday night, drive straight up, and stay in a funny little B&B on the main road into Barrow for £28 a night including breakfast. I'd often arrive at 2am, one of the other residents would have to get out of bed to let me in, and I'd fall asleep with all my clothes on."

After back-to-back meetings all day on Saturday, she'd then drive the 287 miles back to London to pick up her son on Sunday evening.

Despite the exhausting schedule, Nichola was determined to keep self-managing – especially after a disastrous experience with using a letting agent for her Carlisle property.

"When the first tenant moved out, months went by while they couldn't find anyone – and in the meantime I was drumming up viewings from London with my own marketing! Then when I turned up to do a viewing with someone I'd found, the ground floor was in half a foot of water – they'd failed to leave the radiators on low during the winter, and the pipes had frozen and burst. Amazingly, the guy still took it and paid me a £1,200 deposit in cash there and then! I went straight to the agent to collect their set of keys, and that was the last time I'm ever going to give responsibility for my properties to someone else."

Even though she felt better off on her own, self-managing from a distance still wasn't easy. "The main problem was tradesmen taking me for a ride. I only know the basics of construction, and because I was just some Kiwi chick miles away…I must have lost thousands. They all seemed very plausible, but they ripped me off."

"Kiwis in general are quite trusting, open people – the first couple of years I was in London I'd be smiling at people on the Tube and end up with all the crazies talking to me! I sometimes forget that not everyone is as honest as I am, and it's caused me problems. I think the key is to find a couple of people you can trust, and then do business with their recommended people, building a circle of ethical professionals."

Nichola also knew before investing in Barrow that most of her tenants would be in receipt of LHA or Disability Living Allowance – "It doesn't take a genius to look at the unemployment figures and work that out" – which comes with even more management challenges, especially from a distance.

She wasn't deterred, because her time in social work had prepared her for the realities she'd face. "I'm used to dealing with people in lower socio-economic groups, and my job was all about finding solutions with limited resources."

"You have some bad experiences, but you sort them out. I had one tenant who disappeared, leaving dog faeces smeared all over the basement – but immediately I found someone who was so keen to move in ahead of anyone else that he said he'd clean it all up himself, along with the rest of the house. I gave him a couple of months of free rent in return, and everyone was happy."

Moving north

Eventually, a few factors aligned and persuaded Nichola to move up to be near her properties – "And when I decide something, I don't hang about. Within three months of deciding to move, I moved."

The idea had been brewing for a long time. "I was running to stand still. I was paying £950 for the mortgage on my own house and £800 on childcare, while still paying back investors and other bits…I kept thinking about how much money I'd save by moving up to my properties."

By now she had seven properties, and self-managing was becoming more and more of a strain. At the same time, her son was coming up to school age and she didn't want him growing up in central London. "I was working in child protection, so I was seeing kids running around with knives and guns – and I didn't want that for my son. Cumbria has some of the best schools in the country, and luckily my son's father wanted the same thing for him, even though it meant moving away from him."

The final push to move to Barrow was meeting a guy – "and that was the big big mistake".

Nichola met her new boyfriend while she was trying to find a tenant buyer for the property that the elderly couple ended up moving into. "This guy asked me to meet him on the Sunday morning when I was up for the weekend, and I was totally taken in."

"It took only a few months for me to quit my job, rent out my house, and drive up through the snow on Christmas Eve. I thought it was so romantic!"

Although there were several compelling reasons to make the move, she couldn't find a job in advance – and finding any social work position in Cumbria proved more difficult than she'd expected. After two months without an income, she was forced to take a job in Trafford – 94 miles away.

As well as the financial pressure of not having a job, Nichola was paying all the rent and suspected that her boyfriend was stealing money from her. "There were days when I was scrambling around for change to buy bread. I pawned my wedding ring for £500, and all of this was happening over Christmas when there's always a big issue around whether tenants will actually pay up. When he eventually left, I found demands hidden down the back of his chair – there were court appearances I'd missed because I had no idea we even owed the money. I came very close to not being able to pay my mortgages."

"I'd worked so hard to build up these seven properties, and one person nearly took everything away from me. He was an alcoholic and a con artist, and very violent. I've always been very impulsive and laughed about it, but it made me realise that I need to be more careful. I never want to put my son in that position again."

Moving on

Because the missed court appearances ended up affecting her credit record, Nichola hasn't applied for a mortgage since: "I can't face being rejected, but it's OK because it's forced me to keep being creative."

After getting out of the relationship, she was advised by all her friends and family to go back to London – or even to New Zealand. But because of the schools it was an easy choice to stay on in Barrow, make the most of being near her properties, and keep trying to integrate into a community that was naturally suspicious of outsiders.

Nichola eventually managed to secure a social work job in Barrow, and moved into a three-bedroom house nearby that she secured on a delayed completion. "The vendor was emigrating to Australia and wanted to get shot of it, but didn't need the money right away. We agreed to exchange immediately, and I'd pay him in three years – in the meantime, I'm paying rent of £500 which will come off the balance I owe him. It's perfect for me as a place to live, and by the time we need to complete I'll be in a position to get funding again."

Going full-time

Finally, at the start of 2013, Nichola was able to leave her social work job to become a full-time property investor. "I'd always said that it was just a ten-year career. I was nine years in when I discovered property, and ended up staying a few years too long in the end. If you do it properly, it's a job that runs you ragged...it's a revolving door, and it's emotionally very draining."

Since going full-time Nichola has transformed three of her properties from single lets into HMOs, which have the potential to generate a lot more income. "It comes with risks, but I was very cautious and told myself that as long as half of the tenants pay, I'll be in the same position as I was when they were single lets."

In fact, the strategy was so successful that Nichola has leased two more properties from other landlords, turned them into HMOs and has them almost fully tenanted. "I realised that there were a lot of tired landlords who just wanted their rent and didn't have the energy to deal with multiple tenants. There was also significant tenant demand from contractors in several local industries. I already had the systems in place from my own properties, so this approach allowed me to move fast with little capital input. It's just problem solving again."

Case study

Six-bedroom house on Raleigh Street, Barrow-in-Furness

Upfront expenses:

Purchase price: £125,000 in 2010

Gross monthly rental income: £2,295

Monthly expenses:

Mortgage: £358

Council tax: £130

Gas and electricity: £150

Water: £30

Phone and broadband: £25

Cleaning: £64

Insurance: £31

TV licence: £12

Service contract for boiler: £16

Net monthly profit: £1,479

Nichola bought this house in 2010 and put a family in as tenants, but two and a half years later she was forced to evict them due to non-payment of rent. Having been burnt many times before, Nichola decided to look into spreading her risk by renting the property by the room to contractors who would "pay weekly, go home at the weekends and tend to keep to themselves".

Doing so involved creating an HMO, which required getting a licence from the council and permission from her mortgage lender. "Surprisingly, my lender agreed even though it was a breach of the terms. But it was agreed on the condition that I didn't request a further advance. Done!"

Nichola then paid £4,000 to bring the rooms up to a decent standard, a further £3,500 to turn the smallest bedroom into a shower room to meet the requirements of an HMO licence, and she also had to fit wired-in smoke alarms and fire doors throughout. The property has been fully tenanted ever since, with the rooms let for £80–£100 per week including bills ("plus wifi – very important for contractors far from home").

The project had a steep learning curve, but Nichola used her past experience along with lessons learnt from property courses and other investors she met at the local South Lakes Property Meet – "as well as a fair dose of common sense".

"I consider myself to have something of a formula now: the right procedural and market knowledge, the right staff, competitive pricing, reliable tradesmen, a good relationship with the council, sourcers who can get furniture to meet my budget…it's taken a while, but it's been worth it."

"I've also got a waiting list of tenants, as my current contractors often recommend the place they live as well as my other properties to other people they work with."

The future

In the midst of all this activity, Nichola also set up a letting agency with a couple of partners, which now looks after her own properties as well as other landlords'. She believes that many local landlords are ill-equipped to deal with LHA tenants (a big part of the market in Barrow), and she can use the knowledge she's gained over the years to put systems in place to help them.

With her agency filling her properties and a full-time property manager in place, Nichola has finally been able to realise her dream of taking her son back to New Zealand for an extended stay. "I'll be exploring investment options down under, and spending plenty of precious time with my family too. And maybe when my parents will see that I'm making all this money without having to do anything other than send a few emails, they'll finally be convinced that I know what I'm doing!"

Lessons

Transferable skills

"There's a real crossover between social work and the way I've approached property, because it's all just using limited resources to solve problems for people who really need the help."

Get creative

Nichola taught herself about techniques like delayed completions and lease options, and she uses them selectively when it's in everyone's best interest – not as a blunt instrument to apply to everything.

The long game

Investing in properties hundreds of miles away and self-managing was never going to be an easy option, but it was what Nichola needed to do to make property investing work for her. Having done it, it would then have been easy to give up when faced with the realities of a 500-mile round trip, tradesmen ripping her off, then a damaged credit record…but she kept going until she got to a point where she can enjoy the rewards.

Reap what you sow

Nichola wants to make money, but solve people's problems too. She believes that by helping people out, the money will come later – even if you can't predict at the start how that might happen.

Calculated risks

Nichola sees herself as an entrepreneur rather than a business person, because the definition of an entrepreneur is someone who takes risks and finds creative ways to create value. Nichola has taken risks that many people wouldn't be comfortable with, but she's done it knowing exactly what she's getting herself into.

Invest in learning

Loading up your credit cards to pay for seminars that sell you the dream of property riches can seldom be seen as a good idea, but in Nichola's case it worked – because she was ready to do whatever it took to make it a reality. She's continued to invest in learning new techniques, but she just has them in her toolbox for when they'll work – she's not looking for a silver bullet.

Lisa Orme

"It's hard to imagine now the absolute, immediate stop. Properties that had had people traipsing through all day suddenly didn't have a viewing for six months."

In the freakishly neat folders around Lisa's desk are the records of thousands of property investors. It's fair to say that from her home office on the outskirts of Coventry, she has a pretty good overview of the property landscape across the UK.

Lisa's an investor herself, but in recent years she's also become a highly respected mortgage broker. As a result, she's been involved in hundreds of deals (and attempted deals) every year – which means she understands the realities of the current state of property investment better than most.

In the online forums where she's frequently a voice of caution and practicality, Lisa believes she's thought of as boring, or full of doom and gloom. In reality though, she was one of the first people in the UK to use all kinds of exotic strategies – and having survived the worst of the economic fallout herself, she's now in an ideal position to see what really works for building long-term wealth.

Taking flight

Lisa grew up in Birmingham, in the council house her parents had just bought with the help of her nan. For everyone she knew, buying their council house was the limit of their ambition. "I didn't know it was even possible to own a second home. I didn't know anyone who had stocks and shares, didn't know anyone who ran their own business...my uncle was seen as rich because he had a couple of savings plans!"

Lisa always aspired to more, and her mother frequently told her she didn't know where she got her ambition from. From a very young age, this ambition was channelled into one thing: becoming an airline pilot. "I literally cannot remember a time in my childhood when I didn't want to be a pilot. I'd do nothing but read books about flying, and I could recognise absolutely any plane."

Private flying lessons were never going to be an option, but Lisa found a retired pilot who recognised her enthusiasm and took her up in his plane every time she managed to save up £25 from her Saturday job in a supermarket. As a result, she could fly before she could drive. "I've been up on Christmas Day and New Year's Day – there's nothing like being up there when the world's so quiet."

After her A-levels, Lisa was accepted at three universities to study Aeronautical Engineering. She also applied to British Airways for sponsorship through her studies – with the intention that she'd get a position as a trainee pilot afterwards. They turned her down at the medical for being half an inch too short.

"These days my height wouldn't even be a problem, but they were very strict about it at the time. In hindsight, knowing more about my personality, I think I'd have hated being a pilot and would have got really bored. But at the time I was crushed."

Now she knew she couldn't fly, studying the theory wouldn't be the same. She turned down all her university offers and went to work at Lewis's department store in Birmingham.

A life of crime

In 1989 Lisa had been working at Lewis's for a couple of years, and she was bored and lacking direction. Sensing that she should be doing more, she went to the local library on the way home from work one day and headed straight for the careers section. "I took out an A–Z of careers, flopped it open, and it happened to open on the 'Forensic Scientist' page."

"I knew what a Forensic Scientist was – which most people didn't at the time – because my aunt was really into crime thrillers about murders and would lend them to me. So I looked into it, and something about it really appealed to me."

There were six forensic science labs in the UK, and Lisa got accepted by five of them. The nearest was in Huntingdon in Cambridgeshire. "I got a call at Lewis's on Friday from my dad, saying they'd called and wanted me to start on Monday. So we drove there on Saturday, going around looking at all the cards in newsagents' windows trying to find somewhere to live."

The only house she found was shared with a perma-stoned man who was growing cannabis in his wardrobe, and a woman who refused to clean and would take dirty clothes out of the washing basket to wear to job interviews. With little choice, she took it – and stayed there for two years. In 1991 she transferred to a lab back in the Midlands.

From tenant to owner

Lisa's only experience of property was her stint as a tenant in Huntingdon. But in 1992 she met Stuart, her future husband, and they bought their first home together. "We were on holiday in the Lake District, and interest rates were at 12% when we arrived. Then we went into WH Smith and saw a headline saying they'd gone up to 15%. By the time we got to the pub over the road, the barman told us they were now 19% – not great as we had to start paying our mortgage when we got home!"

Rates settled down and Lisa and Stuart were happy in their new home, but over time they became interested in building their own dream house. They spent weekends looking around showhomes to pick up ideas, and Lisa would keep a scrapbook of interior design inspiration. They never thought of property as an asset, or a business, or anything other than somewhere to live – they loved their jobs, and just wanted to build the perfect home.

Then in the late 1990s, a friend of Lisa's from work introduced her to Amway – a network marketing company. Its members sold products directly, but were also encouraged to recruit more salespeople by receiving a percentage of their sales too. "The Amway system itself wasn't for me, but they gave us a lot of motivational books to get us into the right mindset, and that really opened my eyes to a lifetime of reading about business and self-improvement. We'd already started to come to the conclusion that being employees wouldn't allow us to ever get what we wanted in life, and that idea was only reinforced by the books we were now reading about acquiring assets and not relying on a job."

An Aussie awakening

The seeds had been sewn, but the real shift in Lisa's thinking didn't come until a six-week holiday in Australia in 2000. "I threw some books into my suitcase, and by the last week of the holiday the only one left to read was *Rich Dad Poor Dad*, by Robert Kiyosaki. I sat on the balcony and started reading, and couldn't put it down. Everything that had been in the back of our minds was written down on the page – being a business owner, having assets...I could suddenly see how it'd get us to where we wanted to be."

"So I went inside where Stuart was watching the Grand Prix, threw the book at him, and told him not to stop reading until he'd finished it!"

Stuart was similarly inspired by the book. He'd also proposed to Lisa earlier on the trip, so they spent the rest of their holiday planning their lives together and working out how to put their reading into action.

In the course of their conversations, property had come up as something they could do. Back in the UK and filling up with petrol on the way back from the airport, Lisa picked up *Dalton's Weekly* and saw an advert for a manual about how to start a letting agency. Within months, they'd registered a company and were running an agency in the evenings and weekends around their jobs.

At the time there was only one other lettings-only agency in Coventry, so all it took was an advert in the local paper for the phone to start ringing...and it didn't stop. "We were both working full-time and there was a lot of juggling going on, but luckily most people wanted to do viewings outside of office hours anyway. Even so, the whole agency thing wasn't for me – but it allowed me to see that the landlords were making all the money, and we needed to be like them!"

The first deal

For the first time, Lisa and Stuart aspired to owning property other than their own home. As well as the push they'd been given by Robert Kiyosaki, Lisa had realised that their endowment was underperforming and wouldn't be enough to pay off their own mortgage – so they needed to take some kind of action to secure their future.

She sold the endowment for £40,000 ("by sheer fluke, just before they all crashed and you could only get pennies for them"), with the intention of buying one property that could hopefully pay off their own mortgage.

The first property they spotted was a semi-detached house that needed a bit of work doing. "We called the agent, who told us that it wasn't selling because the vendor worked strange hours and they couldn't arrange any viewings. So we said we'd see it any time at all, and eventually secured a viewing for 7am on a snowy winter morning. We were literally the only people who'd been able to see it, so we put in an offer and it was accepted."

They used the endowment money and credit cards to fund the deposit and the refurb, and shortly afterwards they sold it on for a profit of £40,000 – they'd doubled their money on their first deal.

Not surprisingly, they went full steam ahead.

What you know and who you know

Lisa had been nurturing a network of contacts since they first started thinking of buying a property, and was spending her free time educating herself on online forums about different investment strategies. Her education and her network both helped Lisa to do deals early in her investing career that wouldn't otherwise have been possible.

One of her contacts was a developer who'd just had a sale of four new-build units fall through. The developer told her that if she could complete on all four units by the following week – the end of their financial year – she could have them at the same price that the original buyer had reserved them for 18 months ago. Being 2002 and with property prices inching up, this made for a great deal.

"Unbelievably, we managed to complete on all four houses in five working days, using mortgages with the Coventry Building Society. It was a real example of why you should have your team together before you need them – I'd already been talking to the solicitor and the broker for a year, so we were ready to jump at the opportunity when it appeared."

They decided to hold on to the four houses and rent them out for income. "Our first tenant moved in, paid his deposit and first month's rent, then promptly stopped paying and trashed the place.

It turned out he was a 'professional tenant', and had been to prison for fraud – even though nothing showed up on very thorough background checks. So we ended up £12,000 down as a result – and that was our first ever tenant!"

Undeterred, they remortgaged two of the properties to get their deposit back out so they could move on to the next purchase.

Their next purchase was from a lady who was emigrating; she already had tenants in place who used to be the owners but couldn't keep up with the mortgage payments. The tenants wanted to buy the house back, but the husband had only just started a new job so they couldn't get a mortgage for another year.

Lisa gave the tenants an option to buy – effectively a "lease option", which was a tool being used in the US and Australia but virtually unknown in the UK. "Ford had just launched a leasing scheme for cars called Ford Options that was well-known at the time, so I used that as a way of explaining to people about lease options." Two years later, the tenants did buy the property back, giving Lisa and Stuart a profit to take forward into future deals.

Turning pro

With successful deals under their belts and some money to play with, Lisa and Stuart didn't want to give up their jobs but they *did* want to spend their spare time focused solely on investing rather than managing. They closed their letting agency, and passed the management of their own properties over to another local agent – who they still use today.

Then in 2005, their plans changed. Lisa started working for "the boss from hell", who made her hate the job she'd loved for the last 15 years. "One day I had an annual review which was just awful. I came home and Stuart said, 'If you don't want to go back, don't go back.' So I never went back! I called up the next day and said that was that."

With Lisa suddenly full-time in property, their security was reliant on Stuart's income. But the following week, he got a letter out of the blue – the company where he'd worked for the last 17 years had gone bust.

He quickly found another job, but in the meantime Lisa was becoming so busy that in six months' time he had to quit to help her out. So in 2006, with the property boom in full swing, Lisa and Stuart dived headfirst into property.

Riding the boom

Other than flipping their very first deal, they planned to buy and hold on to everything – in line with the *Rich Dad Poor Dad* model of working on your asset column. But after a "lightbulb moment" during a conversation with a commercial finance expert, Lisa came to realise that not all great purchases make great rentals. From there, they sold on any purchases that didn't make perfect sense as a buy-to-let.

"We were doing lease options, land deals, refurbs, buy and sell...you name it, we were doing it. At the peak we were doing between two and four deals a week."

Most of their leads were coming from a big regular advert in the local paper, but they got creative too. "Over the years I've done taxis, sides of buses, leaflet drops, magazines, fridge magnets, beer mats...but the local paper outperformed everything. My dad brought me a huge number of deals too – he'd talk to anyone and he could talk for England, so as soon as anyone mentioned property he was giving out my card."

And with prices rocketing, there were some extraordinary deals to be done.

"There was this one property where the family had moved to the Isle of Man. It was like they'd just had a cup of tea then vanished – the teabags and milk were still out on the side! We bought it for £70,000 on a Friday, went round to see it, and we were so busy with other refurbs we decided we didn't have time to clear it all out and get it ready to rent. So we stuck it back on the market with an agent on Monday, and by the end of the day it'd sold for £99,950. They completed in cash by the following Friday – a week start to finish, and we never even moved the milk and teabags."

Another winning deal was a four-bedroom house in Solihull. "The guy owned it free and clear, and had it on the market for £350,000. I said, "I can't pay more than £250,000 for it because of the stamp duty I'd have to pay," just being honest and not expecting anything, and he immediately said, "OK". It turned out he'd bought it for £90,000 years ago and just wanted to get rid of it, and his wife wouldn't do viewings because she didn't want people in the house."

They put it back on the market for £299,950, and 24 hours later it had sold – making Lisa nearly £50,000 profit in a day for next to no work at all.

Case study

Two-bedroom cottage in Coventry

A deal that Lisa did in 2005 is a good illustration of how she used creative thinking to get a good deal for everyone involved.

As a result of her advert in the paper, she got a call to see a two-bedroom cottage in the outer suburbs of Coventry, because the owners were moving to Australia. The rest of the family had already gone, leaving the husband to sell the house.

He had it on the market for £275,000, but accepted £214,000 from Lisa because he just wanted to get it sold quickly and join his family.

The cottage needed nothing doing to it, but Lisa obtained planning permission for a third bedroom above the garage – just to add a bit of value – then put it back on the market for £275,000 with planning. It was a good deal for a buyer.

An accountant in his mid-20s contacted them wanting to buy the cottage, but he had a two-bedroom flat he needed to sell first. "It was in a nice block, and a great location – just a 15-minute walk into town."

So Lisa bought the flat, allowing him to buy the cottage. "We sold it to him for £249,950 so he didn't have to pay stamp duty, and he effectively funded our deposit for the flat."

Lisa still owns the flat today. Having bought it with none of her own money for £82,000, it's now worth £110,000 and is making a rental income of £550 per month.

By not being greedy and creating a good deal for all parties, Lisa still made £30,000 after costs and ended up with a perpetual stream of rental income.

The honeymoon is over

Lisa and Stuart got married in 2007, and went back to Australia for their honeymoon – the place where they'd had their property revelation just seven years earlier. They came back to find a world that was going mad.

"It was just surreal. In the future it'll be interesting to look back and think we were a part of it: Lehman Brothers, people queuing outside Northern Rock...not a day went by without some kind of financial disaster. And we were stuck in the middle of it – we had properties mid-build, lenders going bust...it was just mad for two years."

Because they'd only ever remortgaged to take their initial deposit back out, they weren't as badly off as many people. "We'd never raped the portfolio for cash, and the properties we were in the middle of selling had flexible bridging arrangements with the

Newcastle Building Society. They gave us enough time to arrange sales, or get them ready to rent out ourselves."

"It's hard to imagine now the absolute, immediate stop. Properties that had had people traipsing through all day suddenly didn't have a viewing for six months."

Fortunately, just before the complete stop imposed by the credit crunch, Lisa and Stuart had decided on their honeymoon to call their own halt on most of their activity. "We never intended to do as much as we did – the plan was only to have a pension, and do a little bit of buy-to-sell to have some income. So we came back from the honeymoon and started to consolidate our finances."

"We got rid of the cars, the magazine and gym subscriptions, the holiday club memberships...even though we had all this money coming in, it was just going straight out again and it had to stop. We sold a few properties to put cash in the bank too."

"I just thank God really, because if we hadn't got married when we did and gone on honeymoon when we did, we wouldn't have taken those measures just in time and we'd have been in a lot more trouble. I don't know what would have happened."

What surprised Lisa the most about the crash was the complete lack of activity in the market. "It was like turning off a tap with the adverts. The exact same adverts that would keep the phone ringing all week would suddenly get one call a week if we were lucky. So there were no deals, no first-time buyers, and you couldn't quickly buy-to-sell anymore because they brought in the rule that you had to own the property for six months before you could get finance. Nothing we were doing was going to work anymore."

It was this lack of activity that Lisa had never anticipated, and it made her re-evaluate her opinions about the market. "In the boom we knew it was a boom, but I always said that if I could make money in that market I'd make ten times more in a down market. The logic made sense – if it's harder to get mortgages, people are going to be more motivated. I was never fazed by falling prices – if I'm buying to hold I'm in it for 30 years, so I could ride it out as long as I could cover the mortgage."

"I couldn't have been more wrong. With no *activity* in the market, there was nothing I could do. In the boom, say you've got 100 people in the marketplace, ten of them are willing to think about selling quickly to me for a lower price, and maybe one of my offers will be accepted. Then suddenly activity stops, and you've only got ten people in the marketplace. Only one of those ten is willing to think about selling to me, and suddenly my chances of getting an offer accepted are next to nil."

Lisa believes that the government is deliberately encouraging this lack of activity, to allow time for the banks to sort themselves out and for property prices to come back under control. "It's well known that the government controls the press for propaganda purposes. If they want to talk up the market it's all this 'My house is going up by £150 a day' stuff, but now they want to talk the market back down. That, and the herd mentality, have created a complete lack of activity. There's this perception that it's all doom and gloom and there are no mortgages and you need a 40% deposit...it's not true, but it suits their purposes to spread that perception."

Case study

Three-bedroom ex-council house in Coventry

"I love ex-council houses because the proportions are just super. This one has three double bedrooms, so it rents repeatedly to sharers. We don't put together HMOs or do multiple tenancies, but if people come together on one tenancy that's fine."

They bought it in 2003 for £83,950 on probate – "It took forever to go through, but we just sat it out." They spent £5,000 upgrading the electrics, putting in a new bathroom and tidying up the garden, and had it revalued at £125,000 – just below the stamp duty threshold.

"We could have sold it on and pocketed £30,000, but it's a great rental so we just remortgaged it to £86,000 to get our money back out and haven't touched it since. It rents for £600 a month."

This model of remortgaging to pull out the deposit but not going any further has been part of Lisa's strategy from the start. It effectively allowed her to buy a monthly rental cashflow for free, without taking it too far and being over-leveraged when the boom ended.

Becoming a broker

In 2009, having restructured her own affairs following the crunch and with the phone still not ringing, Lisa had to find something else to do. Going back to a job was never an option, but she wasn't sure what business to start. She was seriously considering combining her knowledge of forensics with her OCD and starting a crime scene cleaning business, until one day she was chatting to a builder who said she'd make a good mortgage broker.

"It'd never occurred to me, but as soon as he mentioned it, that was it. Stuart and I blasted through CeMAP [the required professional qualification] in a couple of weeks. Then as soon as we qualified, my own broker called me to say he was packing it in. He literally said, "I've diverted my phone to yours – I'm off to run a pub!"

But she couldn't do anything for most of his clients because the mortgage landscape had changed so much, and in 2010 – her first year of being a broker – she only completed one mortgage.

Then in 2011, she realised that she'd not really told any of her online contacts from her years of obsessive forum networking that she was now a broker. She started posting more regularly about finance and mortgages, and the business took off. She's now a trusted authority on mortgage matters in several of the major online property forums.

And while she only ever intended it to be a sideline, she's loving being a broker. "I just feel energised by the whole business. I like research and problem-solving, I love order and uniformity, and I enjoy putting systems in place. There's a lot of overlap there."

One of the privileges of being a broker is seeing first-hand what strategies are being used by a diverse range of investors. And from what Lisa sees, success looks, well...pretty boring.

"The people in the best financial position now and in the future are the ones who've used the simplest strategies: they buy and hold, they rent it out, and they sit and wait for time to take its course."

"The ones in the most trouble are the ones who've used the 'creative' strategies – and it pains me to say that, because I'm a creative person and I've done all this stuff myself. We were among the first to do lease options, rent-to-buy, sale-and-rent-back and all sorts, but they were only ever intended to be tools to be used where appropriate – not taken to the Nth degree."

Indeed, Lisa says that many of the most successful investors she knows just stayed away from the boom completely. They're sitting on their low-geared portfolios, and are starting to buy again now prices are cheaper.

"You've got to learn from others, and learn from history. My own attitude to debt has changed a lot over the years – I see people who are very low geared, and they're doing well. I can't imagine anything worse than lying in bed wondering if interest rates will go up."

A gradual return to normal

Although the mortgage market is coming back ("The rates are terrible and the criteria are tough, but you can get 85% BTL now – that's what everyone was doing with Mortgage Express before the crash"), Lisa thinks it'll be another five to seven years before things are really back to normal.

"By the time rates rise, people need to be able to remortgage and able to sell – the government won't allow rates to go up until that's the case or it'll spark thousands of repossessions. Everyone loses out when there's a repossession, including the banks. It would also damage confidence so much that the economy would collapse again."

When rises come, Lisa thinks they'll come slowly at just 0.25% at a time. "There are people who say you need a big correction and just get it all over with, and there's method in that. It would've been one thing in 2008, but I think it would be incredibly painful to go through five years of nothingness then have a sharp correction. Of course, there will always be people teetering on the edge where a 0.25% increase will wipe them out, but that's always going to happen."

Lisa thinks it'll be 2017 by the time rates reach 2%. "A lot of missed mortgage payments from 2007–2009 will be off credit files by 2017, so people will be mortgageable again."

The future

Lisa admits that she was never enamoured with being a landlord, and although the current market means she can't sell any of her properties, she's optimising her portfolio to be more robust and lower her risk.

"We're going through a process now where every time a house becomes empty, we'll go in and refurb it to get an extra £25–£100 a month and a better quality of tenant. We're arranging things so we can concentrate on working tenants, and we won't have to worry about any changes to the benefits system."

Her plan is to get her portfolio back to what it was meant to be in the first place: a pension.

"When I retire – which I want to do sooner rather than later so we can travel – I want to be in the position of having a small, totally unencumbered portfolio, fully managed, and let to professional tenants. I don't want to be 75 and stressing about what'll happen if a boiler goes or rates go up. We'll do some buy and sell for income, but when the market kicks in again we'll start selling off some of our rentals."

"Ten or 12 unencumbered properties making £750 each in profit per month, plus our pensions and the income from any businesses we own by then...that'd make me ecstatic."

Lessons

Clean your own properties

"I enjoy it – it's part of my OCD – but it also means that you get to see every last inch of your property. Even with the best tradesmen in the world, things will get missed. Just last week I was cleaning between tenants and I spotted a leak behind the en suite sink and a loose tap...little things the tenant would move in and complain about, which I nipped in the bud."

Keep it simple

Lisa uses her creativity for deals and financing solutions, but reins it in when it comes to interior decor. "We provide a blank canvas for them to add their own stuff, then it'll be back to normal when the next people move in. Giving it the full *Changing Rooms* treatment will cost five times as much, and they'll only want to change it anyway."

Develop systems so you can run on autopilot

"We had our guy go and put in some new blinds last week, and we just said, 'Same as last time please.' We didn't have to spend ages picking out colours and all the rest of it. We also use the same colour of paint in every house, so if we need to touch up one wall we've always got matching paint."

More supply means better standards

Lisa doesn't believe that rents have increased that much since she started investing, because the increase in supply was matched by so many people getting into property during the boom. The result is flat rents, but increased standards. "The first rented property I ever lived in was a mess, and that was quite typical. We'd come home and find the landlord sitting in our living room watching telly! You can't get away with that anymore. Whatever you think of the buy-to-let boom, at least it's given tenants more rights and a better standard than they had before."

The demand for home ownership won't go away

"There's less of a stigma to renting now, but there's still the element of 'An Englishman's home is his castle'. Ownership is only down from 72% at its peak to something like 68% now, and I'm already placing people with mortgages who only have 5–10% deposits. Things haven't changed, they've just gone back to how they were – we need to forget about the bizarre period in the middle."

Arsh Ellahi

"I'm coming more and more into the mindset that you don't have to own a property to make money from it, as long as you've got a system that works and can solve problems for people."

Arsh Ellahi and his brother, Aki, have never known a life without tenants, maintenance and huge bunches of keys. As a result, they've got everything down to a ridiculously fine art. Even a BBC film crew, following the brothers as part of a documentary about "benefits landlords", abandoned filming at their office because their business ran too smoothly to make for good TV.

Their father, an immigrant from Pakistan, built up a sizeable property portfolio in Wolverhampton, and the brothers helped him run it in almost every minute they had off from school. Upon leaving university in 2000, Arsh took it over formally – he and Aki concentrated on managing and scaling the family business, while their dad attempted the closest to "retirement" that his work ethic would allow.

The brothers now have 500 tenants living in properties that the family owns, and they run an agency that manages 300 more. All 800 tenants are on benefits – a market that is usually thought of as needing intensive management and causing a never-ending series of problems. Arsh and Aki, though, have *everything* in hand: the phone only rings twice in the three hours I spend in their office.

Empire-building on £3 a week

Arsh's father arrived in Wolverhampton from Pakistan in the 1960s in search of work, leaving his wife to join him at a later stage. He rented a room and took a job in a factory.

He earned three pounds per week. He'd use one pound to cover his expenses, send one pound back to his family in Pakistan, and put one pound aside. After a few years of putting his pounds aside, he was able to buy his first property – a three-bedroom semi – and bring his wife over.

Arsh was born in the UK, the youngest of six children. They couldn't afford the costs of running the house, so all eight family members would live on the ground floor while the upstairs was rented to lodgers. As was typical of the family's nature, they used it as an opportunity to better themselves: "My parents – my mum especially – didn't really speak English, so one of the lodgers taught them."

Now with some security, Arsh's father was able to set up his own precision engineering business – his former trade in Pakistan – and as he made money he'd put it aside to buy more houses. He chose to rent them out by the room, seeing it as less of a risk than renting the whole house out to a family who might not pay.

"The benefits system has been through a lot of changes in between, but in the 1970s it was much like it is now – tenants would get paid in one lump, and my dad would have to go and chase them for it.

He and my mum would be waiting outside the houses for the postman at 6am – and he'd find tenants hiding in wardrobes, jumping the fence with the money…all sorts. It was a crazy time."

"Eventually, the benefits system changed and started to pay landlords directly. He saw this as an opportunity, and bought more houses."

One of Mr Ellahi's earliest purchases was an end-of-terrace house on Wolverhampton's Compton Road, for which he paid £350. Over the next 15 years, other houses on the terrace came up for sale – and as they did, he'd buy them all. He now owns the entire row of eight houses, with seven or eight people living in each one.

"Today, that row of eight houses generates just short of £400,000 a year. And he did it all without mortgages – there was no such thing as a buy-to-let mortgage, and he wouldn't have had the earnings or credit history to get one anyway."

A family business

Arsh's father was determined to instil his own fierce work ethic into his children. While all his friends were playing football, Arsh's school holidays involved working in the family steel factory.

"We'd work from 8am until 12.30pm, come home for lunch, then be back at the factory from 2pm until 5pm. It certainly got us used to the idea of working for a living."

Every Saturday and Sunday morning was dedicated to the property portfolio, and Arsh would help by going into each house to empty the electricity meters. "Every room had its own meter, so I'd go in every week to empty out all the 50p coins. It took bloody hours because I had a huge bunch of keys, and had to try each one in turn until I found the right one! But in the process, I got to know the tenants and learnt the raw basics of multi-letting."

"One of the tenants I knew back as a kid actually passed away earlier this year – and he was still living in the same room in the same property. He lived there for 38 years, and when you think about his rent over the years it would have paid for my dad's whole portfolio several times over."

When Arsh left university in 2000, his dad was in his 60s and ready to have a break. "He was getting on a bit, and he'd been working non-stop for decades. He had a tough time – he was struggling to collect the rents and it was clear that he needed a hand."

"When I took over, I looked at the portfolio from a business point of view, and saw that most of the hassle was coming from the working tenants. I'm yet to find a professional worker who'll be satisfied living in HMO-style accommodation – they always think their rent's too expensive, and they feel hard done by when they're asked to pay each month."

"At the time, the council was paying the landlord directly for 85% of the rent – so for a typical £100 weekly rent, there was only £15 at risk for us to chase. So I took the decision to get rid of all our professional tenants, and dedicate our entire business model to serving people on benefits."

Landlords turned traders

With his father's portfolio refocused on tenants on benefits and the rents being reliably paid, in 2001 Arsh turned his attention to riding the property boom by trading properties.

Arsh and Aki would advertise all over the West Midlands for people who needed to sell their house quickly, and would offer 80–85% of the property's market value to buy it immediately. He'd then market the deal to a list of investors he'd built up from networking locally, and take a finder's fee in the middle.

"When the market was growing, our company was trading up to 30 properties a month. I'd buy on a Friday morning and would have sold it by Friday afternoon on the same day, simply by simultaneously exchanging and completing contracts, taking a £5,000 fee in the middle."

This was the main focus of Arsh's business until, in the face of the emerging credit crunch, lenders started withdrawing the ability to do back-to-back deals, in which properties sometimes changed hands twice in a matter of hours with very different prices. By early 2008, Mortgage Express – the lender that traditionally had the biggest appetite for these deals and asked the fewest questions – became the final company to pull out of the market.

In this new, more cautious environment, lenders started enforcing a guideline from the Council of Mortgage Lenders that they'd previously completely ignored: that lending should be refused on any transactions where the seller had owned the property for less than six months.

A similar rule had existed in the US for a long time, but its introduction in the UK put a complete stop to the model that had served Arsh so well. "We'd have to own the property for six months rather than a few minutes!"

Rather than giving up on the business of buying bargain properties altogether, Arsh and Aki changed their approach: rather than waiting the required six months before selling their deals on, they put tenants in and kept the properties as part of their own portfolio.

The brothers had never planned to be landlords on a bigger scale than they already were, but the new lending rules forced their hand. "By the time we'd done all the hard work of setting the property up and putting tenants in, we figured we might as well keep them and start building things up."

Case studies

One such deal was a property they bought from a taxi driver in "one of the worse areas of Wolverhampton". They paid £40,000 and stripped it back to brick, spending another £20,000 on it. It now generates just under £20,000 per year in rent.

Another property had been on the market with an agent for months, and was already set up as a six-bedroom HMO. It was originally marketed for £150,000, but it had been repossessed and Arsh eventually agreed £102,000 with the lender. They spent £400 on it, and it now generates £27,000 per year.

"These are deals I never would have done before the rules changed in 2008 – I'd have just traded them to another investor and let them handle the headache."

Arsh's biggest headache, but possibly his best deal, was a 17-bedroom HMO in West Bromwich. It was a nursing home which he bought for £500,000 from a distressed seller, with the property already generating £65,000 in rent from the current tenant. Then, the following year, the nursing home company left.

They put the property back in to auction but couldn't find a buyer, and couldn't find another nursing home or housing association to take it on, so they decided to do some work.

"We spent £70,000 putting a kitchenette in each room, adding six extra rooms, and rewiring the whole place so each room was electrically heated from its own meter. The kitchenettes allowed us to set the rent at £100 per week, so the property now generates a profit of £120,000 per year, and we don't have to worry about bills because there's no gas and the tenants have to pay for their own electricity."

Ever-evolving systems

The brothers' portfolio was now growing, but in 2008 they were hit by another change that forced them to change the way they ran their business.

Ever since Arsh had taken over the business in the year 2000, he and Aki had deliberately focused on tenants on benefits because 85% of the rent was paid to landlords directly. But in April 2008, a new system – Local Housing Allowance (LHA) – came into effect, meaning that for any new tenancies the rent would be paid to the tenant, who would then need to pass it on to the landlord.

For the rent to be paid directly to the landlord, the tenant needed to be classified as "vulnerable" – which involved presenting evidence to the council and waiting for eight weeks. "And if the application failed, the tenant would have eight weeks' worth of rent that we were never going to see again!"

With hundreds of tenants on benefits and enough experience to know that the money was unlikely to be sensibly set aside and handed over, the brothers needed a plan to make sure the rent was collected.

Their first solution was to approach their bank for a third-party indemnity account, meaning they could bank the cheques themselves if the tenant signed the back. Getting hold of the cheques before they were cashed, though, involved a strange case of history repeating itself. Just like their dad had to do in the 1970s, the brothers began stalking postmen, knocking on doors, and being given the run-around.

They soon worked out that the cheques were sent on a Wednesday and would land on tenants' doormats the following Monday. So, every other Monday, Arsh and Aki could be found sitting in their car outside the postcodes where they had the most tenants, waiting for the postman.

"We'd wait for the postman to turn up, and as soon as he left we'd knock on the door – but even then, some of the sharper ones had already grabbed the cheque and run out the back door to Cash

Converters. We also got in trouble with the Royal Mail who thought we were interfering with the delivery of the post!" It was clear that they needed a better system.

Their next attempt was to approach RBS, who allowed them to have a mandate to access a tenant's online banking account. "So we made it a condition of business that the tenant would have to open up an account with RBS, sign the mandate, and ask the council to pay their benefit into that account – before they could get their hands on the keys."

"We set up about 30 of those, and it was the best system ever – no chasing postmen, no knocking on doors…we'd just do it in the office at 7am on a Monday, going into one online bank account after another. If a payment had been missed we'd know about it straight away, and we could get right onto it."

Unfortunately, the system didn't last long. "I got a call from the new Regional Manager at RBS; he'd noticed that we had access to 30 accounts and wanted to know what was going on. Even though I explained that his staff had authorised it, his problem was that the money would go in then we'd take it straight out a few hours later – so the bank wasn't making any money! We couldn't leave it in there and the tenants weren't about to start doing any long-term saving, so they shut the whole thing down."

Desperate for a better solution, they hit on another idea – approaching a credit union, which would set up a special account for each tenant's benefits to be paid into and automatically passed on to the landlord. "Wolverhampton Credit Union weren't keen because they make their money on savings, but we pointed out that we'd be willing to pay £5 per transaction for hundreds of transactions each month. We worked with them and helped them get their systems set up, and it started working well so we made it a condition of our tenancy."

"There are professional thieving tenants out there who flutter from one landlord to another, and we quickly learnt to insist on *our* method of payment. Sometimes they'll do it for a week then go to the council and ask to be paid into a different account, but we spot it and get it switched back very quickly. If we own a property ourselves we'll give anyone a chance if we think they're worthy of it – with no other strings attached – but being paid into the account we choose is non-negotiable."

Benefiting from LHA

Finally, Arsh and Aki had found a way of securing their payments. With that sorted, they were able to fully take advantage of a positive feature of LHA – the fact that in Wolverhampton, LHA rates were a lot higher than normal market rents.

Under LHA, the level of housing benefit is set so tenants have access to roughly the 30% cheapest properties available to rent within an area. And because these levels are published, landlords can price their properties at the exact level of LHA entitlement and know that tenants on benefits can afford them.

Due to the size of the areas and the way rents are calculated, the amount of LHA rent is sometimes higher than the open market rent would be.

For example, for a standard three-bedroom property in Wolverhampton, the market rent was £450–500. The LHA rate was

£550, so Arsh could price his properties at the exact rate of LHA and know that any benefits claimant would be able to afford it.

"Now that we'd overcome the problem with payments, we were finally ahead – we'd be making £70 on a room each week instead of £55." It was only new tenancies that would fall under LHA – existing tenancies would continue under the old system – but now they'd cracked it, Arsh and Aki issued new tenancies on all their old pre-2008 agreements to move them over to LHA.

A new kind of agency

The brothers hadn't given any thought to looking after properties for other landlords, but word started to spread that they had a system that worked.

"A family friend approached me because he had a family in one of his properties who'd cashed all their cheques and built up arrears of £1,000 – clearly, months had gone by when he'd not been able to do anything about it. So we took it on, got it into our systems, and before long we were looking after ten properties for him. We weren't charging him because he was a family friend, but it made me think that there was something to do here."

Rather than operating as a traditional agency charging a fixed percentage, Arsh decided not to charge any management fees at all, and just offer to pay the landlord the standard market rent.

"We'd take a property on for the normal market rate of £400, and rent it out to people on housing benefit for £600–700. We were making a few hundred quid each month and had everything down to a fine art, whereas a normal agency charging 10% would only make £40 for running around, doing all the viewings and chasing money!"

Using his in-depth knowledge of the benefits system, Arsh can sometimes generate even more profit. "We had one family turn up on our doorstep who had three kids aged over 17, all on housing benefit. The parents were entitled to the one-bed rate, and each of the three kids was eligible for the shared-room rate. In total it added up to £270 per week, so that's the rent we charged them. We were only paying the landlord about £115 a week, which was the market rent for a four-bedroom house, so we were making big money."

The council sometimes challenges this model, but hasn't been successful because Arsh is playing exactly by the rules. "There's nothing illegal or immoral about it because everything's fully disclosed to the council. We're not even creating an HMO because they're all related…we're just making use of their allowance."

The agency has been using this model ever since, and now has over 300 tenants on its books. "It's great – we're making good money so we don't have to bother collecting top-ups from the tenants, and everyone's happy. We're making as much from 100 properties as other agencies would from 600–800 properties."

It's somehow fitting that their systems are only so robust because LHA forced them to change the way they do business several times over, and those robust systems are now allowing them to make every property highly profitable by exploiting the LHA rules.

"We've come on a journey – a great journey. Provided you've got a decent system, there's no reason to have any rent arrears. I'll go out and see landlords who are £3,000 in debt, and wonder how they let things get to that point. We can boast 100% rent collection now."

Arsh is now applying this system to a rent-to-rent model too. "We'll guarantee the rent for ten years, so to my mind the commitment on my side is exactly the same – I've got a commitment to pay the landlord each month instead of the mortgage company. But the difference is that it costs me no legal fees, no valuations, no need to spend months going through the rigmarole of the whole process…a landlord can come in today and it can all be done tomorrow."

"I'm coming more and more into the mindset that you don't have to own a property to make money from it, as long as you've got a system that works and can solve problems for people."

Understanding Wolverhampton

Arsh has spent his entire life in Wolverhampton – "a funny little place" – and isn't hopeful about its future.

"Wolverhampton got city status in 2000, but since then it's only become worse. Unemployment is high, and the city centre is struggling – two out of every three shops in town are empty. One problem is that the council isn't very forward-thinking: they had investment opportunities from Irish backers, but they all fell through because the council wasn't forthcoming with ideas and incentives."

High unemployment is good for business though, and Arsh will steadfastly defend his tenants when anyone talks negatively about the benefits sector: he did, after all, decide to build his entire business model around benefits tenants because they were causing him less trouble than professionals.

"We refuse to tarnish our tenants with any kind of stigma: if I lost everything tomorrow I'd be on benefits, and I'm under 35 so I'd only be eligible for a single room in a shared house. Our tenants have brought us to where we are today, so we give them as many opportunities as we can."

One such opportunity was given when Arsh got a call on a Friday afternoon from a family who'd been living in a tent in Kidderminster for a year. "I didn't have anything to offer them, but I persuaded another one of our landlords to take a risk on them. It was a risk, but something told me that it'd work out. I called the guy back and told him to be at our office on Monday morning, and six years later they're still living in the same house – they've been the best tenants ever."

"You can't reference-check someone who's been living on the street. Our general rule of thumb is you have a chat with them, get a feeling about them, then take a risk. When we were first tenanting our 17-room place in West Bromwich, we had a lot of rooms to fill – so we went out and approached charities and housing shelters. You're going to get people who're down on their luck, but most of them don't cause you any grief."

Most of them, but not all – and on one occasion Arsh had to go out to the 17-bedroom West Bromwich property at 3am. "It wasn't even the tenant, but her daughter's boyfriend was nicking the copper piping and flooded the room because he cut the wrong pipe. I wasn't too impressed, and at 3am he didn't find me in my calmest frame of mind. You've got to lay down the law though, because if you get one bad egg who starts acting up, things can escalate very quickly in a property of that size."

Arsh believes that the most important trait for a landlord operating in his sector is "hard skin".

"You've got to be prepared to hear every lie and every threat under the sun. You get tenants who tell you they're going to burn your house down...all sorts. If you're afraid of confrontation, this line of business isn't for you. If you've had tenants build up big arrears, it's probably because you're scared to confront them."

But like with any type of business, there are good and bad customers – and over the years, Arsh has learnt to avoid problems by screening out problem tenants at the application stage.

"Over time you get good at sizing people up. In general, if you take on a scumbag you're going to have problems from day one and they'll continue causing problems throughout the tenancy. If you've made an error of judgement, you need to spot it straight away and get them out as quickly as you can."

The future

With systems finely honed and two members of staff to carry them out, Arsh has been able to escape the day-to-day tasks of managing hundreds of tenants, and focus on the strategic side of the business.

"I'll talk to the banks, sort out the correspondence for purchases, deal with the odd issue like benefit payments that have been suspended...but not much. The phone hardly rings in our office, because by now we've worked out how to put the right tenant in the right property, and employ systems that work from day one."

Arsh is now working on plans to help others benefit from those systems, by franchising the letting agency He's also working on growing DSS Move, an online portal that he and his brother have built to help people on benefits find suitable properties.

"With Rightmove, most properties aren't available to people on benefits – but there's no way to check other than to click into each description. We used to list our properties on Rightmove, but found we hardly got any enquiries because most people on benefits had just given up looking. So we've built our own portal where every property is available to people on benefits, and it's great for landlords who want to attract that type of tenant because it's completely free to use. We've got 10,000 properties listed on there and get 50,000 visitors a month at the moment, but we want to be getting 100,000 visitors and cover every postcode in the UK."

Arsh is 33 now, has just had his first child, and plans on retiring by the time he's 45. He's using the profits from everything except the family's own portfolio (income from the agency, rent-to-rent and property trading) to pay down his debt – he wants to retire owning everything free and clear with all the cashflow he'll ever need.

And when that happens? "I'll probably start a new business, or I'd get bored. My father put a hell of a work ethic into me, so I don't think playing golf for 40 years is really an option."

Lessons

Keep utilities separate

Perhaps as a result of spending his childhood emptying the 50p coins out of electricity meters, Arsh never includes utilities in with the rent. "I've been out to properties where they're included, and they're heated like a sauna in the middle of summer – with the window open. And you can't do anything about it because you can't be seen to be withholding heat."

Organisation is key

"Our office is a calm, harmonious place because our systems take care of pretty much everything. And they all start with who you put into your property – if you put the wrong person in, you're going to have problems the whole way through."

Work hard, work smart

"If you're scared of hard work, this sector isn't for you: a lot of landlords would have fallen at some of the hurdles we've come across. We've done waiting for the postman, we've battled with the banks, we've worked with credit unions…we've come across all these hurdles, and because of the work ethic my father put into us, we wouldn't give up when we hit them."

Don't put things off

"If something needs doing, do it quickly. It keeps tenants happy, and a tenant who's happy in their property will stay longer – with 38 years being the example."

Gavin Barry

"It's more important to me to be free of debt by the time I'm older than it is to have everything I want now. I'm just seven years into a 20-year plan to eliminate my debt."

On 4 January 2004, Gavin Barry sat in a McDonald's in Liverpool having breakfast. Outside, everything he owned was packed into his car. Aged 28, he'd just left behind his life in London – including his flat, his City job and his girlfriend – based on nothing but his belief that Liverpool had great times ahead, and his desire to claim a part of it. He planned to invest in property, even though he had no capital and just about enough in his bank account to cover nine months of living expenses.

He remembers his overriding thought that morning: "Oh shit."

Nine years later, he owns a portfolio valued at £6.5 million, generating rents of £40,000 per month. He also owns a letting agency, a development company, and a company that sources deals for other investors. His aim: to generate as much cash as possible, and to own his assets debt-free by the time he's in his early 50s.

Gavin clearly has a taste for the finer things in life – he's immaculately dressed, drives a nice car, and has recently come back from an extended overseas break. But he's by no means profligate – which soon becomes clear when he starts telling his story. He's happy chatting over a burger in a student cafe near his office, and he's only just moved out of a two-bedroom flat into a rented house because his first child is on the way.

A calculated risk

If someone told you they were leaving their life behind to start again in a city they'd only visited once for a football match, you might think they were having some kind of breakdown. In Gavin's case though, there was an impeccable logic behind his decision.

Four years previously, he'd been browsing the *Sunday Times Rich List*, and noticed that 70% of its members had made a large part of their fortune from property. So with property seeming like a smart move, the only question was "Where?"

Gavin knew that Liverpool was receiving EU money from the European Objective One Fund, and he'd seen the regenerative effect that the same fund had achieved in his native Dublin. Liverpool had three universities and an enduring tourist and cultural appeal, yet property prices were relatively low. That, in combination with the Irish connection and being a Liverpool FC supporter, was good enough for him.

Rather than writing a plan for his own business, he wrote one on the city itself: essentially a 25-year bet on the future of Liverpool. It was enough to convince his landlord's brother Oliver, a successful developer who wanted to branch out from London, to put up some money and go into business with him. So in 2004, Gavin moved to Liverpool and Oliver followed him – both convinced of its prospects, but still not exactly sure what they'd do to grab their piece of it.

Early entrepreneurship

The sudden fixation on property was new – it had never been a childhood interest, and even now he considers it a vehicle for freedom rather than a passion – but the drive to make money on his own terms had been with Gavin from early in life.

Aged nine he would cut pictures out of the *Smash Hits* magazines that his mum would buy him, and sell them to his friends for 5p. He also washed cars, walked dogs, washed windows and mowed lawns before hitting the jackpot: running the school shop.

He'd load up his mum's car at the cash and carry, and supplement the typical sweets and crisps with an under-the-counter product line: cigarettes, bought in duty-free cartons from his sister who worked for Ryanair, and sold on at a 100% mark-up. Intent on reaching a wider market, he'd even employ other boys and give them boxes of product to sell from outposts elsewhere in the school.

"I think the drive to make money must've come from my grandfather, who was an entrepreneur himself and was always quizzing me about how my little businesses were going – he got a huge kick out of encouraging me. Even in those days though, it was never about money for its own sake – more about the freedom it could buy me."

Perhaps it's surprising, then, that Gavin went on to study Accountancy at Dublin Business School. "I liked accountancy because you were either right or wrong – I never liked shades of grey. But I could never get my head around taxation – as much as my tutors told me to suspend common sense and just learn the rules, I couldn't do it."

As a result, he failed his final year and never went back to complete it – by that point he was off travelling the world, after which he settled down in London and began working in financial PR. "I never loved my job, but I didn't hate it and I loved the London lifestyle. I was making good money and having a lot of fun, but it was only a matter of time before my entrepreneurial instinct kicked in again. I needed to do my own thing."

Arriving in Liverpool

Having arrived in Liverpool, knowing nothing and nobody until Oliver moved up, Gavin started networking. He met a local investor who put up the money to buy and refurb a three-bedroom house in south Liverpool; Gavin did all the work, and they split the profit. After that first deal, Gavin was busy but not focused: he bought run-down terraced houses in unpopular areas; bought land, got planning permission and sold it on; bought houses, got planning permission to convert them into flats then sold; and did conversions himself to sell on.

The model was to buy, add value, then sell. Not every deal made a profit, but Gavin and Oliver were making progress. Even so, they were risking their capital every time: Gavin still didn't have the passive income he'd read about in the *Rich List* that inspired him in the first place.

Then in 2006, they bought ten off-plan flats just as the market began to turn. By the time the flats were completed, they couldn't find buyers: they had to forfeit their deposit on eight out of the ten, taking a loss of £90,000.

Rather than declaring bankruptcy, they gradually traded their way back to zero. But Oliver was disillusioned and moved back to London. For Gavin though, that wasn't an option: returning to London would have meant admitting failure, and he was determined to see his plans through to success.

To earn some capital he took a job working for a local developer – which gave him some guaranteed income after three years of slog with nothing to show for it. More important than the company car and the £70,000 pay packet, he received an education in property investing – commercial property in particular.

With this newfound knowledge but still no real assets of his own, Gavin was more motivated than ever to start building his own portfolio. So in March 2007, for the second time in just a few years, he quit a job that gave him a good income, frequent holidays and nice cars, to start all over again.

Building a portfolio

Having quit a comfortable, well-paid job once, doing it again wasn't a big deal: he'd come to Liverpool for a reason, and he knew it was time to start building up his assets.

Once resolved to building his own portfolio, Gavin took action – and bought 14 properties in a year. He compensated for his lack of capital by persuading investors he'd met while networking to lend him the money to buy distressed properties. He'd then use Mortgage Express' same-day remortgaging product – a tool used by many investors at the time – to instantly remortgage for a higher value and pay his investor back.

He bought with a view to refurbing and renting out, and in one case transformed a three-bedroom flat above a shop into a six-bedroom flat with a hairdresser on the ground floor. He also bought seven small blocks of LHA flats. In every case, the intention was to buy and hold, seeing the surplus rents as the passive income he'd always wanted.

Then though, the credit crunch hit, and his entire approach changed again.

Getting serious about debt

As with many investors, the financial crisis and the lack of credit caused Gavin to stop and take stock. While the previous years had been about building an asset base, the crunch caused him to look a lot more carefully at the level of debt he'd taken on. "I was lucky to be young enough to see what was happening to those around me, see that debt is a terrible thing and can destroy people who don't manage it carefully, and be able to adjust my plans accordingly."

Although he'd not taken any drastic risks, he could see many people in his network lose everything as a result of being over-leveraged – "and if interest rates had gone up more quickly, I would have been one of them. Even now, a rate increase of just 1.5% would wipe out the majority of investors."

The game had changed, and now his mindset was all about generating cash and paying down debt – not just accumulating everything he could. At this point, he began focusing largely on student properties: because HMOs generate such large amounts of cash, he could use the surplus to overpay on his mortgages.

"I'm typically overpaying £800 per month on a £300 mortgage – that way I can get my 85% mortgages down to 75%, and refinance on better terms. In the meantime, the recession is doing me a favour because my debt's being inflated away."

Really, it's an exercise in delayed gratification. "It's more important to me to be free of debt by the time I'm older than it is to have everything I want now. I'm just seven years into a 20-year plan to eliminate my debt."

Why students?

Gavin focused on student houses for two reasons: they generated lots of immediate cash which he could use to pay down his debt, and the student cycle was predictable enough that he could systemise, delegate, and free himself up to work on other things.

"When you're dealing with professionals, they're highly mobile – they're always moving in and out – so you can never stop marketing, doing viewings, reference checking, and so on. With students, you know that they're all going to move in and out at exactly the same time. That means you get into an annual marketing and maintenance cycle – I know exactly when my busy and quiet months will be, and I can put systems in place to deal with it."

Looking at one of Gavin's HMOs, it's clear that he's honed his systems effectively. Every house has a manual including every last detail a tenant could ever need to know – down to how to use the washing machine, what day to put the bins out, and the location of the stopcock. "It's easy to forget that students are just kids – many of them have never done anything for themselves, and they don't have a clue how to use a washing machine. By having a manual, they can just look it up instead of calling us every five minutes...although in practice they call us every five minutes anyway, and we just tell them to look in the manual!"

Because everything's so highly systemised, Gavin barely needs to be involved once he's bought a property. He employs an in-house project manager to supervise refurbs, and has precise instructions for what the quality of the end product must be like – even down to having artwork on the walls, ready for students to move in and have it feel like home. Marketing, viewings and referencing are handled by staff at his letting agency, and regular inspections ensure that someone can take care of any issues before they become major problems.

Gavin is only interested in big HMOs with five bedrooms or more, because those are the properties that generate the returns he's looking for – typically a return on investment of more than 25%, and a net profit of at least £1,000 per month.

He's also got a strict set of criteria when he's buying. "I'm always looking for two social spaces – a decent living room, and a kitchen that's big enough for a table and chairs. That way, if one group wants to watch TV while others are drinking and getting ready to go out and party, they're not going to be in conflict with each other. And a lack of conflict means they're more likely to stay on for another year, reducing our workload. Another thing I aim for is equal-sized bedrooms – again, it's easy for resentment and arguments to set in if someone's got a bigger room than someone else.

The art of the deal

Like all serious investors, Gavin always wants to get a good deal:
buying at a good price improves yield, makes for instant equity,
and protects against any short-term falls in capital value.

By focusing on a small area and knowing it in intimate detail,
Gavin's able to know exactly how much to pay for any given
property, acknowledging that "Sometimes, the best deal you can do
is to walk away."

He'll find potential purchases through his local network and also
through auctions – although he'll never buy in the room.

"Auctions are a great source of deals, but I'll always try to secure a
deal before it goes to bidding, or afterwards if it didn't get sold.
There's too much irrationality in an auction environment – you can
end up bidding against amateurs, or people who're looking for a
house to actually live in, who people who have a totally different set
of criteria and can bid prices beyond anything that makes sense to
me."

Whatever the source, doing a deal comes down to being able to spot
an opportunity, and having the confidence to follow it up even
though no one else has snapped it up already.

"A good example is a building that had a shop on the ground floor
and a flat above. It had been in an auction catalogue that went out
to 5,000 people, and it didn't get sold in the room. I think no one
wanted it because the shop was on a pretty weak commercial
parade, but I knew I had a good shot of getting planning permission
to convert the ground floor into residential."

"I took a chance and bought it at a great price, but my first planning application was rejected. I knew someone further down the road had already done it so I applied again, and it was accepted. Now it's an eight-bed student house that's making me a profit of over £1,500 per month. More than 5,000 people saw that opportunity, but only I had the confidence to take advantage of it."

Case study

Seven-bedroom house on Granville Road, L15

This is the house that Gavin picked up in 2011 after it failed to sell at auction with a guide price of £150,000. He paid £115,000.

"It was a prime example of how you can always spot an opportunity if you know your market better than your competition does. This one is on a corner plot, which is always good for HMOs because you've got more windows – so you've got more options to reconfigure the space."

He converted the ground floor commercial space into a new layout that allowed for an eighth bedroom, an extended kitchen and a new lounge space.

On top of the new layout, Gavin installed a new central heating system, rewired the house to install emergency lighting and a new fire alarm system, and installed a new kitchen, bathrooms, and a new laundry room. He also fully redecorated – which involved re-plastering, new floorboards and new carpeting.

Upfront expenses:

Purchase price: £115,000 in 2011

Refurb costs: £45,000

Legal, finance and survey fees: £4,000

Gross monthly rental income: £2,833.33 (8 bedrooms x £85 per week x 50 weeks)

Monthly expenses:

Mortgage: £593 (70% LTV at 5.93%)

Gas, electricity and water: £332.66

TV and broadband: £29.99

Insurance: £20.80

TV licence: £12.08

Maintenance fund: £250

Net monthly profit: £1,594.80

Gavin put £40,000 of cash into the deal, giving him a return on cash invested of 47.8%. He's happy to leave his cash in the deal, and will be using the lion's share of the profits to pay down his debts in line with his long-term plan.

Knowledge is power

Because Gavin knows that you need expertise to spot deals that no one else can, he's gone to great lengths to develop that knowledge through thousands of hours of book-reading, internet research and seminars. Another source of information is other investors and property professionals, and Gavin goes to great lengths to build his network, travelling the country to speak at events and running a popular monthly meeting in Liverpool. "I consider myself lucky that networking comes naturally to me – I love people, I love helping people, and it just so happens that by helping people without any expectation of getting anything in return, you end up stumbling across opportunities."

Having stumbled across those opportunities, the next step is having the confidence and determination to both act on them and see them through even when things are going wrong. "I've worked hard on developing a positive mindset. You've got to develop a bulletproof shield against bad news – if you don't get planning permission or a property gets downvalued, you can't take it personally. You've got to keep on fighting, and work out what you're going to do about it."

Daily routine

Rather than living off his rental profits, Gavin is focused on using rental income to pay down his debts and using other ventures – like his letting agency and sourcing company – to fund his lifestyle.

The focus on cash has also seen him go back to his buy-refurb-sell roots. "I've got a series of joint ventures happening now just like I did when I started: another investor puts in the money, I put in the work, and we split the profits 50-50."

These activities keep him busy. "I'm up at 5.50am every day, and at my desk at 6.05am. I get up to 100 emails every day, and it takes me until 9am to process everything. After going through my emails, I make a list of the 10–15 people I need to call that day, so I can keep the list with me and squeeze in calls whenever I get some downtime."

After that it's a full day of driving around Liverpool: viewing sites, inspecting houses, going in and out of his solicitor's office, meeting brokers and lenders, talking to surveyors, builders and architects...the mix changes depending on the stage at which his projects are at, but there are always people to meet.

On top of that there are meetings with his staff, project managers of deals in progress, and investors to raise more money. In the evening, if he's not at a networking event, he goes home to deal with the less urgent emails he didn't get to in the morning.

The future

Gavin sees himself as being five years into a plan that will see his family debt-free and with a large asset base within 15 years – and with his first child on the way, security is more of a priority than ever.

He talks about handing over the rest of the day-to-day running of the business and moving back to Dublin, or maybe applying the lessons he's learnt to starting up a new business in a totally different area. Whatever he does, it's hard to imagine Gavin doing anything other than what he's done since he was nine years old – work hard, make money, and have fun while doing it.

A property investor's inbox

Gavin broke down for me the typical themes of the hundred or more emails he receives every day:

- Up to 20 emails a day from solicitors, depending on how many transactions he's got on the go and at what stage they're at

- Investors

- Potential new investors

- Accountants on structuring deals and various issues connected with the four companies he runs

- Council officers on council tax exemptions or revaluation requests

- The manager of his management company/letting agency

- His project director updating him on individual projects

- Finance brokers on either financing or refinancing his most recent deals

- Joint Venture partners

- Coaching and mentoring clients

- Emails from people who've read his magazine articles or seen him give a presentation

- Random property emails from land agents and deal sourcers (most of which "are crap!")

Lessons

Perfectionism will hurt you

It's just not possible to build a sizeable portfolio, run a letting agency and take on development projects on the side if you're still the one unblocking the toilets and answering the phone to tenants – yet many property investors find it hard to cede control to someone else.

"I struggled with perfectionism for a long time," says Gavin, "but two years ago I finally got comfortable with the idea that if I could train someone to do something to 90% of my own standard, that'll still be acceptable for me."

"It involves a lot of work at the start, answering questions and correcting the process, but it's worth it. I now meet with the girl who runs my letting agency once a week for half an hour, and I that's enough for me to know about everything critical."

Offer incentives

Gavin recognised that if you want someone to behave like a business owner, you need to treat them like one. "In every area of my business I identify an employee who wants to take on more responsibility, work out a revenue share with them, and leave them to get on with it."

Play the long game

Even though his portfolio is generating £40,000 in cash every month, Gavin relies on other streams of income (like his letting agency) to pay his living expenses. He's attained the passive income he first wanted when reading the *Rich List*, but is deferring the rewards by paying down his debt.

It's not what you know...

Gavin is naturally outgoing, and he's in his element working the room at a networking event. He knows that having a large network will bring opportunities his way, and he builds that network by helping people and teaching what he knows. The personal gain is a happy side-effect.

Resilience counts

Even after taking a £90,000 loss on a single deal, Gavin worked his way back to zero, and from there to a portfolio that generates nearly £500,000 in rental income every year.

"You're going to get kicked in the bollocks every so often, but you can't take it personally – instead of sitting and crying about it, you've got to work out what to do to fix it."

There's no substitute for hard work

Working from 6am until midnight most days might not be many people's idea of freedom, but it's clear that Gavin enjoys the hustle and has his eyes set on a goal many years in the future – just like he did when he first wrote his business plan on Liverpool's future.

Importantly though, he's not chasing his tail and getting bogged down in details. By working hard on the bigger picture and motivating others to take care of anything that can be systematised, Gavin makes sure that he's propelling forward – not just treading water – at all times.

Kim Stones

"I'd buy at 12.00pm, remortgage at 12.05pm, and have an extra £20,000 in my bank account by 12.30pm. Daft? Maybe, but everyone was doing it at the time."

"When you grow up on a council estate in Doncaster, and your parents named you Kim," he says, fixing me with a steely stare, "getting good at martial arts is a pretty sound move."

Now in his early 50s, Kim Stones is still in Doncaster. But since his schooldays he's become a Tae Kwon Do world champion, travelled the world, gone on to build up a portfolio of 80 properties in the local area…then nearly lost everything when the credit crunch hit.

But you don't become a world champion by giving up without a fight. When it became clear that the world had changed, Kim changed too – and in the process stumbled on a controversial new approach to generating cash from property that's now being used (and debated) all over the country.

Kim lives in an old (and possibly haunted, he thinks), idyllically situated farmhouse about ten miles outside the city, with his wife and daughter. While endlessly friendly and hospitable, and (by his own admission) no longer in fighting shape, Kim still projects the impression of a man you wouldn't want to mess with. He has the typically northern trait of cutting straight to the heart of a matter that makes him endlessly quotable, and he speaks quietly with passion and focus for several hours non-stop.

From Denmark to dojo

Kim was born in 1961 in Kalundborg, Denmark to British parents (his dad was working on an engineering project there), and lived there until he was seven. "All I remember now is it being very clean and clinical. I must've spoken the language I suppose, but these days all I know are a couple of swear words."

School doesn't start in Denmark until the age of seven, so when Kim's family moved back to Doncaster he found he was already a couple of years behind everyone else. As a result he struggled with reading and writing, which is perhaps why he never "took" to academic subjects in general. He loved sports, though – despite not showing much aptitude for them. "I was always picked as linesman when we played football. That meant people didn't rate my footballing skills, but I didn't know that at the time – I just loved running around!"

The family home was on a council estate in Thorne, Doncaster: "A salt-of-the-earth place, but rough." A victim of bullying and finding it hard to fit in, Kim was drawn to the TV show *Kung Fu*, starring David Carradine –the first show to expose the Western world to martial arts. Without telling anyone, he quietly started training in Tae Kwon Do.

Before long, even though no one knew what he was doing, the other kids sensed that they should stop picking on him. "It gave me an inner confidence that I'd never had before. I knew I could handle myself, and that must have shown through."

Kim's teachers saw his dedication and encouraged him, turning a blind eye when he'd skip lessons to train, and giving him the keys to the gym on the quiet. Their faith paid off: he earned his black belt at the age of 16 – one of the youngest in the UK to do so at the time – and was picked for the World Championships in Oklahoma when he was 17.

That was just the start. He travelled all over the world competing, and while officially still at school, Tae Kwon Do came first – he skipped his final Economics A-level exam because it clashed with the European Championships. His biggest regret of the time is that he didn't win the championships – the lack of A-level doesn't cause him much angst.

The teacher appears

Kim kept competing while holding down a day job at a factory in Doncaster – Young's Seafoods – and dating Coral, who became his wife.

All he really wanted to do was teach Tae Kwon Do professionally, and even though martial arts weren't big in the UK at that time, he saw his national coach teaching in the Midlands and knew he could do the same. "It's a good life lesson: if you want to do something, find someone who's already doing it and get their advice. People will help you if you just ask."

In 1979 he started his first school, charging 50p per lesson to teach a few local kids in a church hall. His attendance slowly grew, but he was still working a shift pattern in the factory and had to "feel ill" every Wednesday afternoon to get out to teach his class. Eventually he had to leave the factory, which gave him the impetus to build his class further.

By the time he stopped competing professionally, 15 years later, Kim had won the World Team Championships three times and had been the World Individual Champion in 1991. And significantly for the next phase of his life, he had built up his part-time school to the point where he was teaching 100 students who paid him £3 per class. It was time to channel his competitive spirit into something new: turning his school into a proper business.

A lesson from America

In 1995, while Kim was on holiday in Orlando, he was amazed to see about 30 full-time martial arts centres next to each other on University Drive. That was all the motivation he needed to believe that it could be just as big in the UK,

Soon after, he went to New York to train with a martial arts school there. He came back and started copying their methods in staff training, systems and marketing: "There's no genius to it – just nick it and import it." The most important shift was putting students on monthly contracts – like they do at gyms – which changed their mindset and got them to make martial arts training more of a commitment. It also gave him a predictable monthly revenue.

When he first started insisting on monthly contracts, half of his students left immediately. Having 50% of his students quit at once wasn't comfortable, but Kim stuck with the monthly contracts. "They hadn't seen what I'd seen, and I knew it'd work."

Before long he had two full-time schools: one in Doncaster with 520 members grossing £25,000 per month in fees, and another 1.5 miles away in Armthorpe with 200 students generating fees of £15,000 per month.

The property bug bites

While Kim had been building his business, he'd also been dabbling in property. In 2000 he'd bought his first buy-to-let property, and used the equity in his own house to slowly buy more until he had ten. "In those days you could remortgage your house and they'd literally give you a cheque book to spend the equity!"

He kept running the schools, but the property bug was gnawing away at him. In 2005, the opportunity to sell the schools appeared, and he took it. While the transaction went through, Kim thought more about property and realised just how much freedom it could create.

In June 2006 the deal to sell the schools completed for just under £500,000, with payments structured over a period of many years. With a regular income and no school to run, Kim had the time and motivation to start accumulating properties faster.

He advertised extensively – with leaflets and ads in the local paper – to people who wanted to sell their properties quickly at a discount to market value. Then, as was a common technique at the time, he'd remortgage based on its full market value on the same day as completion.

Effectively, this meant Kim was using his portfolio as a cash machine. "I'd buy at 12.00pm, remortgage at 12.05pm, and have an extra £20,000 in my bank account by 12.30pm. Daft? Maybe, but everyone was doing it at the time."

In the short amount of time he had before the credit crunch kicked in, he built up a portfolio of 80 properties using this method – mostly residential, but some commercial.

"At the time I was sitting there doodling five million, ten million in assets on a bit of paper – it looked realistic at the time because everything was going up so fast and we were buying so much." He was buying purely to remortgage and use the cash to pay his living expenses – he passed all the management over to a local agent, and the rental income would just about cover the mortgages.

Then in 2007, as Northern Rock fell and the media was full of stories of meltdown in the credit markets...Kim just kept going. He was still out advertising for Below Market Value properties, and as each lender closed their doors he'd just move to a new one. The closure of Mortgage Express cut off his biggest source of finance, but he still managed to do a few last deals with Chelsea Building Society.

Finally, everything stopped – meaning no more purchases, and therefore no more cashbacks and no more income: "It was like a tap had been turned off."

It wasn't just the lack of income – Kim also had an expensive bridging finance obligation he had to meet. "I was in the middle of buying a plot in Thorne with a commercial unit downstairs and flats upstairs, and I'd exchanged with delayed completion. While we were waiting for completion, the Northern Rock collapse happened, and the banks just pulled everything. I could have pulled out and settled the matter for less money than it ended up costing me, but I wanted to protect my credit rating. In the end I had to arrange bridging finance at 1.5% per month, and kept it going until the bridging firm went bust in October 2011."

The cash generation game

With no more income and fearful of an interest rate increase that would have turned most of his portfolio loss-making, Kim was suddenly playing a different game. Now, his properties couldn't just be an excuse to make a lump of cash from remortgaging – he had to put his assets to work to generate cash for his family to live on. "Every property in my portfolio was now an individual business, and I had to go through and ask, 'What is this property doing for me?'"

Kim acknowledges that he was saved by the interest rate staying low, because it gave him the time he needed to reorganise his portfolio and find ways to make more rental income. "You've got to find a plan. And if that plan stops working, find another plan."

Almost overnight, Kim was forced to move from being the archetypal "big picture" investor to getting into the messy hands-on business of lettings. He pulled his entire portfolio back from the letting agency to save on fees, drafted in his wife and daughter to help with the management, and started converting as many properties as possible into HMOs to boost the income they were bringing in. Although it gave him more income, converting the properties also cost a lot of money. "Before long I'd worked out the magic words with the council: 'Is that the minimum legal requirement?'"

Many of his new HMOs were in areas most suitable for renting to tenants on housing benefit, meaning Kim quickly had to make judgements about who to take a risk on. In the rougher parts of Doncaster, letting it be known that you're a former Tae Kwon Do world champion can be a useful way of making sure you get paid.

Discovering rent-to-rent

While looking for ways to generate more income, Kim came across lease options: the strategy of taking a property from its owner, covering their expenses and renting it out to a tenant, then having the option to buy it for an agreed price at some point in the future.

Kim dived in, but "landlords aren't daft". Even though lease options are widely used by investors and he did manage to complete a couple, he found that he was losing potentially cash-generating deals because landlords didn't want to give him the option to buy at today's price in five years' time. But as Kim says, "You've got to get over it and find a solution – there's always a way."

Kim's lightbulb moment came in April 2009, when he was speaking to a landlord on the phone about a potential option deal in the middle of town – a property with five rooms and a separate flat. "Motivation is everything, so I went over there and we kept chatting until I found out what was motivating her. It turned out her husband had died and left her a lot of money – all she wanted was to go off around the world with her new boyfriend without worrying about the property."

She wanted the property completely off her mind while she travelled, but didn't want to sell it – so Kim just skipped the "option to buy" part. He assured her that he'd take it for five years and she'd never hear from him with any problems, and offered her £500 per month – well below the normal market rent. She took it, and the property is now netting Kim a profit of £1,000 per month.

Kim now has 14 properties on the same sort of deal, which has come to be called "rent-to-rent". "They'll all go back to each landlord eventually, but that's OK – in the meantime I'm generating cash which I can use to pay down my debt or build up my own portfolio." He also instructs other investors how to replicate his rent-to-rent strategy – which generates more cash while making the most of his teaching skills.

Case studies

Five-bedroom house with a self-contained flat in Christchurch Road, Doncaster

Upfront expenses: None

Gross monthly rental income: £1,979 (£75-80 per bedroom per week, plus £100 per week for the flat)

Monthly expenses:

Rent paid by Kim to landlord: £500 (guaranteed for five years)

Total bills: £400

Maintenance allowance: £50

Net monthly profit: £1,029

This was Kim's first rent-to-rent deal, which he took on in April 2009 when he noticed that it had been advertised for sale for a long time at too high a price. He stuck a note to the porch window saying he'd like to pay a guaranteed rent for five years with all the bills and repair costs covered, and it didn't take long for the owner to call him back.

"It's in a cracking location, and it cost me nothing to set up because it was already an HMO – it even had all the beds and wardrobes. I just spent £35, and within two weeks the whole thing was rented."

"This deal is the perfect example of why motivation is key. It's essential to let the landlord talk and get them to tell you why they want to do the deal: once you know that, you know what offer will make sense to them."

Three-bedroom house in Zetland Road, Doncaster

Upfront expenses:

Refurb costs: £1,000

Gross monthly rental income: £1,623 (£75 per week for each of the five bedrooms)

Monthly expenses:

Rent paid by Kim to landlord: £550 (guaranteed for five years)

Total bills: £350

Maintenance allowance: £50 per month

Net monthly profit: £673

Kim pays the landlord the same £550 per month that they would get if they rented it out as a single let. His only costs were £1,000 to put in smoke alarms, fire doors and give it a coat of paint, as well as converting both reception rooms to give the house a total of five bedrooms. "The key here was the kitchen, which is big enough to serve as a communal space and allowed me to get five lettable rooms out of the house. The numbers wouldn't have worked nearly so well otherwise."

"It's not really in the HMO area of town – more on the outskirts – but it's a nice house so it rents very well. We always allow for two weeks' worth of voids in all our properties when we're running the numbers, and we rarely go over that."

How the rent-to-rent model works

As landlords all over the country are turning their attention to generating cash rather than banking on capital growth, many are diving into rent-to-rent – and controversies have emerged about specific legal and practical aspects of the approach. Kim just sees it as solving a problem: it helps the owner of a property who doesn't want to be a landlord, and it solves his own cashflow problem. There can be ramifications if either the landlord or the investor doesn't fulfil their obligations, but that doesn't mean the approach itself is flawed – it's just a tool for solving a particular problem.

Kim says that rent-to-rent can work anywhere in the country. He aims to pay 70% of market rent in return for taking it on for the long-term, but he's willing to pay full price if the numbers still work for him. The key is realising that the landlord just wants nothing to do with the property – so Kim never calls them with problems, and will even go so far as to install a new boiler if it makes sense to do so.

The tricky part is that it's not always easy to make contact with the landlord of a property that's being offered for rent, so Kim has to go via the letting agent – who often struggles to understand the concept.

"You should never mention rent-to-rent, because they won't know what you're talking about and will just turn off. Instead, point out the benefits: guaranteed rent, long-term, and they can have their commission even though you'll be taking care of everything and there'll be zero communication...it's an attractive proposition, but you have to actually point this stuff out rather than rely on them making the connection."

Even then, they'll often be wary about pitching a non-conventional idea to their landlord. "If they say the landlord turned you down, ask if they actually spoke to the landlord – even say, 'What, you spoke to them directly? What did they say?' You've got to make sure your message gets through."

Importantly, Kim was already running a large number of HMOs, had systems in place, and knew his target market. Rent-to-rent isn't something that an amateur should just dive into in the expectation of making easy money.

Competitiveness and communication

When asked if he learnt anything from martial arts that he applies to his business, Kim replies, "Everything."

The most important thing, as you'd expect, is competitiveness. "I never thought I was a competitive person outside martial arts, but I recently realised that I am," he says. "But it's a controlled competitiveness. That comes from my training."

Used to practising the same move for hours on end, he also works harder at overcoming his weaknesses than most. "Like communication – I come across as a good communicator, but it's not natural – I have to work hard at it. I know how important it is to generate a team atmosphere, so I've worked at it."

Communication skills come in useful with problem tenants too. "If someone's not paying their rent, you can't just go mad at them. You've got to communicate with them – '*Why* aren't you paying your rent?' There's always a reason behind things, and you should try to understand the reasons. I don't *like* it when someone doesn't pay or they trash one of my houses, but I don't become emotionally affected by it in the same way that others might."

Kim misses the motivational aspect of martial arts teaching, which is why he's so happy to offer advice to other investors. "I like to get into someone's psyche and help them to become more successful – and there's an art to knowing when you've got to go gently and when you need to give someone a bit of a hard time. I want to say to people, 'There's not much difference between me and you.'"

The future

After his frenzy of acquisition from 2006 onwards, Kim's now turning his attention to consolidating and restructuring his portfolio into something more sustainable in time for when he retires. "If I owned just ten properties without mortgages, that's £7,000 per month before tax to live on when I retire. That's enough for me." He's also getting his daughter Chelsea more involved in the family business, opening up a town centre location for a letting agency that she'll run and own a share in.

Even though he's stopped the expansion, he's far from stopping. "If freedom means not doing anything, I don't want freedom."

Lessons

Start small

"If I was starting again now I'd do HMOs from the start, with a mixture of repayment and interest-only mortgages. But I'd always advise starting small and seeing if you're psychologically cut out for it. When I open the door and see that the boiler's been nicked and the place is a tip, I have very little emotional involvement. Would you be able to put up with that? Would your missus be able to? People want things in black and white, but it's about what works for you: what you're able to cope with, how you want to structure your life, what you want to do."

There's no such thing as passive

"People say that they want to make £20,000 per month, *passive*. And maybe you can get there...eventually. But before you get there, you have to go through this bit here – it's not going to happen overnight. Even then, there's no such thing as truly passive – even passive income needs some maintenance. Even if your properties are managed, you need to be beating up your agent to make sure they do their job properly."

Always think about the exit

"If you buy an HMO in a typical town centre HMO area, you can only sell on to other investors or have all the cost of converting it back. If you buy out of town in more residential areas, you can convert them back into family homes when you want to offload them – I've got some in Wheatley Hills in Doncaster like that. Always be thinking about your exit from the start."

Look for successful people, and model them

"Sometimes you assume that something won't work, but when you look beyond your immediate assumptions and *really* see what's possible, it makes you realise you can do it. For me, going to America and seeing what they were doing there made me realise my business could exist on a totally different level from what I'd always assumed."

Fairness is everything

"I don't put any stock in contracts. Are you really going to sue someone? Are they really going to sue you? I'm straight with people, I'm honest with them, and I'm not going to do 'em. If I go to them with that attitude, what are they going to do to me?"

Success doesn't mean showing off

"There's too much talk of passive income, and going 'Look at me, I've got a Ferrari.' I did it myself when I was running the schools because I wanted to show the instructors what success looked like if they worked hard. Nowadays I don't believe that you need to show that much to convince people – I'm not comfortable with it."

Don't be obsessed with buying below market value

"If it takes a year for you to find somewhere at a certain percentage below market value...well, if you'd just bought somewhere a year ago you would have had 12 months of making £1,000 per month out of it."

There will always be risks

"You've got to eliminate all the risk you can, then accept what's left. And failure is OK – failure means you've had a go at something. The attitude to failure and bankruptcy in the UK is harmful."

Work on your weaknesses

"I'm naturally lazy, but because I'm aware that's a weakness I know how to force myself to do things. I put myself into a position where I've got leverage over myself: when the pain of not doing something becomes greater than the pain of doing it, I'll act."

Be aware of people's motivations.

"Whether you're dealing with a tenant who won't pay, or an agent who won't put your offer to a landlord, or a landlord who won't accept your offer...there's always a reason for them acting like they do. If you understand people's reasons, you can put things to them in the right way."

Mat Smith

"If I'm walking past an estate agent's window and they're listing properties for sale and to let, I can just knock off the last two zeroes and barely slow my pace."

Mat operates with military precision. He meets me at "twelve hundred hours" on the dot, having sent an impeccably organised collection of background materials in advance. And once we've shaken hands, he explains that he's arranged for a driver to take us on a carefully planned tour of Leipzig – an area where he and his colleagues have invested for the last few years.

The precision (and the polished shoes, and the "short back and sides") is explained by the fact that Mat actually *was* in the military – first as a junior technician in the RAF, later rising to the rank of Officer before retiring to become a full-time property investor.

But Mat was never just a military man. He studied for a Physics degree while working in a demanding job putting bombs on planes, then dived headfirst into property – buying 30 properties in the space of 18 months while working in the RAF, and earning financial freedom for him and his family as a result.

He also has a knack for investing in areas where property prices more than double in value within a few years of him arriving. It's a skill that he developed completely without tuition – instead relying on a homebrew investment philosophy that actually disregarded capital growth completely.

Early enterprise

Growing up in Southampton, Mat was "a bit of a scallywag". He also had an entrepreneurial streak, and these two tendencies intersected in his first business venture while still at school: copying computer software onto C90s with a tape-to-tape machine and selling them in the playground.

While stuck at home for a couple of weeks with German measles, he attempted to expand his business by taking out an advert for his pirated wares in a national computer magazine. "My mum suddenly got 300 envelopes addressed to 'Southern Software'…and even though I've got two siblings, she knew to come straight to me. She made me stop, so I got 300 stamps out of it but that was about it."

Mat left school in 1986 without many qualifications, and continued dabbling with businesses "on the fringes of legality" until an RAF brochure landed on the doormat. "There was no forces background in my family, but my dad was insistent that I went for an interview. He realised that I was probably going to end up in prison relatively quickly, and I think I appreciated that he was trying to save my skin – so for once I listened to him."

Despite an odd job interview ("I couldn't name any planes other than Concorde"), he was accepted, and joined as "the one who put bombs on planes" – a role which took him around the world for ten years.

An accidental landlord

Mat had only been in the RAF for a year when he met his first wife on holiday in Majorca. Together, in 1989, they bought a house in Reading. Mat was only 20 at the time, and the experience "taught me lessons I try to remember to this day".

For Mat's first six years of property ownership, its value steadily fell – leaving him in negative equity. So when the military moved Mat to an overseas posting, Mat had no choice but to rent it out and become a very reluctant landlord.

"Interest rates were 15% at the time, and my mortgage was £536.11 – I remember it very clearly because my wages were £610! The rent just about covered the mortgage, but I was still working nights in a supermarket alongside my RAF job to stay above water."

"But then interest rates started coming down, and the rent began to cover both the mortgage *and* my beer in Germany! I suppose that was my 'clang' moment about property: someone else could pay my mortgage and leave me money in my pocket too. That was 1996, just before Blair came in, so all in all not a bad time to be having a 'clang' moment about property."

By 1999 the house, which had been in negative equity for years, had finally increased in value. Mat and his wife had split up by then, so he sold the house and ended up making a £60,000 profit. That £60,000 ended up being the seed capital for everything he's done since.

A well-disguised stroke of luck

Mat married again, to Anna – who was also in the military – and together they bought a house in Grantham for its proximity to several RAF bases.

In 2003 though, Mat was transferred to the north of Scotland – "A stroke of luck, although it certainly didn't feel like it at the time" – while Anna stayed in Lincolnshire.

The stroke of luck revealed itself one Saturday morning when Mat went into Aberdeen to do some shopping, and happened to stop outside an estate agent's window. He noticed that there were flats being sold for £20,000, which were being rented out for £280 or £300 per month. Although he didn't know the meaning of the word "yield", he couldn't help noticing that the rents were extremely high in relation to the capital value of the property.

Essentially, Mat spotted that the Scottish market had become decoupled from the rest of the UK. Prices in the whole of the UK fell from 1989 to 1996, but whereas they recovered strongly in the UK from 1997 onwards, in Scotland they'd just stood still.

"When I first saw these £20,000 units I assumed there must be something wrong with them – otherwise the locals would be buying them. But that's not always the case – a lot of people had been burned before because they bought and saw the price fall for years and years, so they just weren't interested."

"As an outsider I could see that this was a huge opportunity – so I formed a plan to take advantage of it."

Exit strategy

Mat's business plan was simple, but highly ambitious: "I knew that I needed to make an income of £4,500 per month in order to give up full-time work. I could buy properties for £30,000 that would give me a net monthly income of £150. So I needed to buy 30 properties to hit my income target."

"I was up there for 18 months, so we needed to buy about two properties per month in order to be financially free. And that's exactly what we did."

Mat got his first ten loans from RBS, who happily gave out 80% mortgages because Mat and Anna were both making good money from their full-time jobs.

With 80% financing, they needed to raise £180,000 in cash for deposits in order to buy 30 properties. They started with £60,000 from the sale of Mat's house in Reading, remortgaged their house in Grantham to raise another £50,000, and funded the rest from their salaries.

As well as abundant supply, rental demand was strong too: Aberdeen was experiencing an oil boom, and that brought immigrants who weren't too fussy about where they lived. "I started out by thinking 'Would I want to live here?' for every purchase, but as time went on we bought some dirt cheap ones – real Old Kent Road stuff – and they're the ones that really went up in value."

Mat still didn't know what "yield" meant, but "I looked at the numbers and the rents covered the mortgage two to three times over, so that was good enough for me." And because his plan involved buying a lot of units quickly, he didn't bother negotiating particularly hard – or indeed at all.

"You'd see the locals viewing these properties for £30,000 and saying 'Hmm, I'll give you £27,000 for it,' and we'd go in and offer the full £30,000 and give him a bottle of champagne when it completed. He was probably still getting less than he bought it for years ago, so we could at least try to be a bit nice about it. We were only in it for the monthly income, so a few quid off the purchase price was neither here nor there – we just needed to buy a lot of units, quickly."

"We were in a rush, so we just barged into every estate agent in town and tried to buy everything from anyone. We would have got better deals if we'd taken the time to build relationships with two or three agents and worked only with them, but I didn't understand that at the time – and we didn't really have time for getting matey with them because of work anyway."

Seeing it through

Mat's days as an RAF Officer were long and exhausting, and his nights as a property investor saw him driving 60 miles to Aberdeen to bring his new properties up to a lettable standard. "I'd come back to the mess to have a few beers and tell people what I'd been up to, and no one really knew what to make of it. None of them were doing anything similar at all."

Once a property was ready to let, everything was passed to a local agent because Mat was stretching himself thin just keeping on top of acquiring properties and doing his day job.

Having the odd buy-to-let on the side is one thing, but Mat's acquisition programme was so audacious and draining that one would assume he had an extremely compelling motive for acting so quickly. After all, a lot of people would ideally like to leave their job, but most don't commit so fully to a plan that will help them do just that – and Mat enjoyed his job anyway.

"Leaving the military was part of my motivation for sure: I had kids by that point, and I didn't want to be going off to war. But other than that, I just do things for fun: meet new people, make a bit of money…it was hard work, but I loved it."

Being in such a rush did have its drawbacks, and Mat made one slip-up when the end was in sight. "I got a bit brave towards the end of the empire building, and stupidly bought a flat without viewing it. When I got the keys and went over there I had to step over two people having sex, and it turned out there was a mother and daughter prostitute outfit operating next door with customers going in and out at all hours. I didn't sleep a wink that night."

In the end though, he was rescued by the buoyant market – which in itself was a hint that it was time to call a halt on the buying.

"I rented it to a fisherman – you could rent anything in Aberdeen at the time – but I just couldn't be doing with it and put it back on the market a year later. By then the value had more than doubled: we bought it for £30,000, and a woman offered to buy it from us for £80,000. I knew she'd find out about the prostitute next door and I wanted to be a bit nice – although not nice enough to actually put her off buying – so I reverse-negotiated her down to £65,000. That would give her enough leeway to put it back on the market and make a quick profit for herself if she wanted to get out when she found out."

"That whole incident was my cue to say, 'Right, this is getting bloody stupid – these prices don't make any sense. I'm not buying anything else in this city.'"

As it happened, by the time he managed to offload his flat of ill repute, he'd already met his original target of 30 properties generating an income of £4,500 per month. This was the income he'd always known would allow him to quit his job, so in 2006, he did.

Rather than retiring though, a second career as a full-time property investor was about to begin.

A full-time investor

Mat was happy to leave the military because he never saw himself as the kind of person who suited full-time employment: "I never should have had 'a job', and then suddenly I didn't anymore, and I was very happy about that."

Of course, having set up enough of an income stream to support his family, he could have just ceased working and found something else to do. "But who's going to stop once they've hit their goal? You'd become a pretty horrible person if you just sat back and collected rents like a miser, so I threw all my energy into being a full-time property investor."

To raise the funds for the next phase of his investing life, Mat almost accidentally realised that he could remortgage his entire

Aberdeen portfolio while maintaining a reasonable loan-to-value ratio. He'd been buying units for £30,000, which by 2006 were worth between £80,000 and £100,000 – so what was originally an 80% mortgage had fallen to nearer 25%.

"It hadn't really struck me until I went to remortgage one of the units so I could raise money to buy something elsewhere in the UK. The surveyor didn't even go round – he just asked me on the phone how much I thought it was worth. This particular one we'd bought for £20,000 and I said 'Er…£60,000?', expecting him to say 'Yeah right!', but he just accepted it."

"That night I thought, 'Hmm…if I make another 29 phone calls like that…', and that's exactly what I did." After refinancing his portfolio, Mat had well over a million pounds in cash to start his career as a full-time investor.

The increased mortgages meant higher interest payments which put a dent in the monthly income he'd been aiming for all along, but he was confident in his ability to invest the money to make even more. And although he didn't know it at the time, the sudden drop in interest rates to 0.5% only a year later meant that the "base rate minus" deals he'd remortgaged onto left him with only an admin fee to pay.

German skirmishes

The reason for the sudden drop in interest rates was, of course, the financial crash that hit in 2007. "If I'd known what was coming I would've sold everything, but even keeping hold of it I was very lucky to remortgage and get the equity out when I did."

With the UK in turmoil and the housing market having effectively shut up shop, Mat turned his attentions elsewhere.

"I'd just left the military, I had a lot of time on my hands, and a million quid burning a hole in my pocket. I started looking elsewhere in Europe and soon settled on Germany. I'd lived there for a bit about ten years previously, but that wasn't really a factor. The main thing was that I could tell it was in a different part of the cycle from the UK – they hadn't experienced the boom we had. I knew there was a strong rental market because the majority of people rent there, and the legal system seemed robust."

So Mat booked an EasyJet flight from East Midlands airport, and started viewing properties in Berlin.

The property market in Germany as a whole had sat out the boom that had occurred in much of the rest of the Western world. Germany's boom had happened in the 1990s, following reunification, and the bubble burst in 1996. Prices fell for five years until 2001, just as markets in the rest of the world were growing at their fastest. They then stabilised, but had still only experienced very modest growth by the time Mat arrived in 2006.

Despite being in a totally new market and dealing with people he didn't know in a language he didn't speak, Mat wasn't daunted. "I suppose I just thought I knew it all, and there was a bit of exuberance involved because of the run-up I'd had in Scotland. And the cars were worth more than the apartments! How wrong could it go? I suppose I also sensed that we were in a hotspot and needed to buy quickly."

In his haste, a large chunk of his money was spent in one transaction, paying £750,000 for 20 1950s ex-social housing apartments in the suburb of Reinickendorf. "It was a reasonable deal, but I was in too much of a rush – I could have bought so much better."

As Mat's knowledge of the market and his network of contacts grew, he started to learn how to get genuinely good deals. But by then the market in Berlin was showing signs of becoming overheated.

"So I took a small profit and sold up, jumped on the train for an hour, and ended up in Leipzig. There, there was no indication of investors getting carried away – in fact, there were precious few investors at all. It was almost like they rolled out the red carpet as soon as we got off the train, because we were a rare breed showing any interest in buying there. That's usually a good sign, wherever you're investing: do you get the VIP treatment from agents, or are they just not that interested?"

Discovering Leipzig

Mat was attracted to Leipzig for the same reason that he'd been so excited when he stumbled across Aberdeen: high yields, and a market almost completely overlooked by investors.

"Leipzig had an increasing population, oversupply had been worked through and old stock had been demolished, there was easy access to finance, and the city had been effective in creating new high-tech jobs. Also, only 15% of properties were owner-occupied, compared to nearly 50% in the rest of Germany. The home-buying culture was just starting to take root with people in their 20s and 30s, which hinted at the opportunity in the future to divide up buildings and sell them to owner-occupiers at a significantly higher price."

Once again, Mat swooped: over the course of a few years he bought 40 units for himself, plus probably as many as 100 more as joint ventures with RAF colleagues and others. He bought entire apartment buildings rather than individual units, allowing him to scale quickly. At the peak of his activity he had an office in the middle of town, and spent a few days each week having meetings and doing viewings before flying back to his family in the UK.

Having a large portfolio in another country never worried him. He built up his own trusted team of property managers, and management in Germany is less intensive than in the UK: apartments are supplied unfurnished, and tenants have more of a homeowner mentality as they tend to stay in the same property for years or even decades.

By 2012, prices in Leipzig had risen by an average of 60%, and as had happened in Aberdeen and Berlin before, Mat realised that the property market was showing signs of overheating. The cycle in the UK, meanwhile, seemed to have reached the point of property prices bottoming out.

With the opportunity to make his money work harder in the UK, as well as wanting to spend more time with his family, Mat began the process of selling his Leipzig holdings and bringing his five-year stint of activity in Germany to a close.

Case studies

Two-bedroom apartment on Ritter Strasse, Berlin

Mat bought this 63 square metre, two-bedroom apartment for
€52,000 in 2007. It came with a long-standing tenant, and
secured him a "so-so" yield of 7%.

In December 2011 he sold it, with the same tenant still in
occupation, for €87,000 Euros.

"The deal was OK, but I benefited from good timing on the way
in. I could have secured much better deals if I'd been more
professional in my acquisition."

"It's gone up another 50% since I sold, but never look back! Just
keep planting seeds in more fertile earth."

Block of nine apartments on Bornaische Strasse, Leipzig

In September 2009, Mat bought this block containing nine
apartments, an office and a restaurant. He paid €450,000, using a
70% mortgage at an interest rate of 3.8%. Originally he was
trying to sell the deal on to his local and international contacts,
but as no one wanted it he bought it himself.

In December 2012 he sold the building to a local investor for
€665,000. Mat had been collecting a yield of 12% while he owned
the property, but as rents remained static and the capital value
rose, Mat used the compressed yield as a signal to sell the
building on because the market was heating up.

An "embarrassingly" simple formula

Mat's first serious property acquisitions in Aberdeen were driven by gross yield: the annual rental income divided by the cost of purchasing the property.

Although he hadn't come across the term at the time, he had an intuitive understanding that it made sense to buy a good stream of rental income at a cheap price. "I just wanted to replace my income in a sustainable way. That meant getting rental income – so I wanted to buy as much rental income as I could, as cheaply as I could."

Mat has been guided by yield ever since. "I want to buy properties that won't need excessive maintenance, in areas with strong tenant demand, and achieve a yield of 12%. If I'm walking past an estate agent's window and they're listing properties for sale and to let, I can just knock off the last two zeroes and barely slow my pace."

In other words, if a property was being advertised for sale at £120,000, Mat would need to see it commanding a monthly rent of £1,200 to justify taking a closer look. £1,200 multiplied by 12 is £14,400, and £14,400 divided by £120,000 gives a gross yield of 12%.

"It's almost embarrassingly simple, but my whole investing career has been based on that idea. The only clever bit has been finding those investments and managing them effectively."

But while Mat was aiming for income, he was surprised to discover that something he'd never given much thought to – capital growth – had outstripped his rental income by 700%.

"I was giving a presentation at a London property exhibition, and I was trying to make the point that rental yield is the only game in town: capital growth isn't a goal you can aim at, and that's always been the case. It wasn't a message that anyone was particularly excited about hearing at the time – a bloke literally dozed off in the front row – but while preparing to give my presentation I was amazed to calculate just how much capital growth I'd experienced while all I was aiming for was income."

What Mat had unwittingly discovered was that by buying in fundamentally sound but unloved areas, he could achieve high, stable yields. Over time, if the right conditions were in place, more investors would be attracted by the yield, and move into the area. That would have the effect of increasing property prices. In effect, this meant that high yields were a "signal" of capital growth to come.

Of course, high yields don't always point to capital growth: either the yields might be unsustainable and rents might fall due to lack of tenant demand, or other investors might never enter the market. Mat believes that for investors to be attracted to an area, in addition to high yields, there needs to be ready access to finance and general "investor confidence" – which could come from economic improvements, falling unemployment, or positive media reports.

Although Mat has effectively "locked in" his rental yield at the point at which he bought, he uses the compressed yield (meaning that the rent has stayed the same while the value has gone up) as a signal that the market might be reaching its peak. "I've only got one spreadsheet for my entire business – and it doesn't even have multiple tabs! One of the columns in that spreadsheet is 'disposal price': when the yield has compressed to a certain extent, it's time to sell and benefit from the capital growth that's taken place. Because I didn't buy it just to put a picture of it on my wall; I bought it to make money from it, and if that's happened then it's time to move on."

This unemotional buying and disposal of properties, rather than buying and holding forever, makes Mat unusual among property investors who are normally loathe to sell an asset that puts money in their bank account every month. In effect, his approach is similar to the philosophy of "value investing" in the stock market: buying shares in strong but unloved companies that pay a healthy dividend through the holding process, then selling them once other investors notice the value, push the share price up, and the yield is no longer so compelling.

Back to buying British

Mat started building a portfolio in Germany because he recognised that it was at a different point in the property cycle. Now, he's disposing of his German portfolio and buying in the UK again because he believes that their respective positions in the cycle have reversed.

The notion of property cycles that Mat subscribes to was first asserted by Fred Harrison – a British economic commentator who predicted the 2008 crash with uncanny accuracy from as early as 1998. Harrison wrote that the property cycle lasts for 18 years: growth in years 1–7, a small correction mid-cycle, accelerated growth in years 9–14, and declines in years 15–18.

The four phases became known as Stealth, Awareness, Mania and Blow Off, and Mat believes that Berlin and Leipzig are now entering the Mania phase just as the UK is finishing the Blow Off phase and moving into Stealth. "The guy has research going back 400 years to prove his case. I think he approaches it as some kind of socialist warning about the evils of land ownership, but ho hum!"

Mat is currently dividing his time between Leipzig (where he's selling off his portfolio), and the UK – where he's been researching the investment prospects of different cities. It's a research process that correlates suspiciously highly with the route map of the East Coast Mainline. ("What can I say? I like sitting on trains.") He's bought around 25 units so far, geared to 70%, and thinks he has another ten still to go – targeting Leeds, Edinburgh and possibly adding to his Aberdeen holdings again.

Mat has already put himself in the right place at the right time at several points in his investing lifetime, and seems confident that prices in his target areas have fallen to a point that make for attractive investments while maintaining their rental demand. "Every day I spend hours trying to challenge what I'm doing and prove myself wrong, because it seems a bit obvious. But I can't think of a better play."

In Leeds he's buying flats in blocks that were newly built in 2006, and in some cases have fallen 50% in value since. "The price history gives me some comfort – knowing that someone was presented with all the sales brochures for various developments and decided to buy this one, paying significantly more for it than I am now. And I'm making sure that tenants still want to live there now."

"These are luxury units, which really shouldn't be returning a profit to an investor. I mean, how often do you get cashflow when there's a concierge downstairs? That's a good indicator for me."

Getting things done

Mat has clearly achieved an extraordinary amount, and his explanation is that he's developed the capacity for getting a lot done by juggling two things at every point of his life.

"When I was first working in the military I was also working in a supermarket in the evenings to pay my first mortgage. Then I had a busy job putting bombs on planes, but I was also studying for a Physics degree at the Open University. Then I was an Officer in the RAF who was buying 30 properties in 18 months. Then when I left the military I had both things taken away from me, so I had a lot of spare capacity – allowing me to buy lots of units quickly, and help other people out too."

He also acknowledges that his wife has played a large role in everything he's done. "The whole 'behind every great man' thing is very true for me – it's all thanks to her. Before I met her I knew a few things, but I did absolutely zip with it. To this day she keeps me straight about what I buy, and I'd never dream of buying anything without asking her first."

Being a military man, Mat maintains a strict routine. "Up at 6am, do all the banking, get the kids to school, go for a run, come back at 10am. Every day the same. Then the rest of the day there's some management and research to be done, but I've got a lot of spare capacity. Every day is like a Sunday to be honest, but you do need to have spare time to think and really plan stuff."

Now that Mat is consolidating his portfolio back in the UK, he's spending a lot of time on the road visiting properties and doing research. Beyond that, his main plan is "to spend more time bringing up the kids, so they know who their dad is".

"Then, according to Fred Harrison, flog everything in 2022. Another ten years or so to have a good play, then maybe it's time to stop and do something totally different."

Lessons

Buy where no one else wants to

Being the only person buying in an area is a scary position to be in because it means you're either ahead of everyone else or completely misguided, but it's been the key to extraordinary capital growth for Mat.

Buy prime assets

Mat buys up prime assets at bargain prices whenever the opportunity arises. "When it's doom and gloom and the world's going to end, that's the time to be buying up distressed prime assets. I had a dabble in Orlando, and I bought the very best properties so even if the city depopulated by half, people would still want to rent my units."

Focus on yield

"Capital growth isn't a goal you can aim at – if prices had stayed flat I'd have been happy, because I was still getting my income. But if you buy high-yielding properties and folks want to live there, capital growth will naturally come your way."

Make sure high yields are realistic

"Look at places like Buffalo and Detroit: they're just fantasy yields, because no one wants to live there."

Emulate others

Mat figured out his investment style for himself, then refined his system by learning from other investors with far bigger portfolios than his. "If you haven't walked the path before, walk the one that's already been walked."

ᴗna Thompson

"We all want doctors and pharmacists and airline pilots as tenants, but we're never going to get them because they've got their own houses. You're always going to end up with the slightly odd people at the bottom, but the odd people at the bottom can be more reliable than the people at the top."

When you think of HMO properties being rented out to the most vulnerable people in society, you might think of whole families packed into single rooms, "beds in sheds", and tenants living in fear of being illegally kicked out by their cold-hearted landlords.

You probably don't think of a landlord who drives her tenants to hospital appointments, lends them money and helps them to organise their lives. That's what Serena regularly does, even though she had absolutely no aspiration to be a landlord until it was forced upon her. Now though, her unique approach to the job is helping her to work her way out of a situation that could have ruined her.

Serena manages 29 rooms across four houses in Eastbourne, which she lets out to a unique assortment of individuals – half of whom don't work, and many with seemingly intractable personal issues – who've become a surprisingly central part of her life. Her blog, *HMO Landlady*, should be required reading for anyone who's ever tempted to think of property as a purely numbers game: the stories she shares are extraordinary, and she'll pepper her conversation with references to being threatened by a Kosovan Viagra dealer like it's just one of those everyday things.

We sit and chat in the living room of the small, bright terraced house that she shares with her three spookily well-behaved children and her less well-behaved dog. The house used to be one of her HMOs before she moved her family in – "A guy died in what's now my bedroom...well he died in hospital, but he'd lived in his own filth up there for his last few weeks."

Serena's story doesn't appear to have much in common with the others in this book, but really it's about freedom through property just as much as the others are. Although she'll readily admit that property got her into quite a mess in the first place, it's now allowing her to have a good life with her kids as she works her way back to zero.

Falling into property

Serena's husband worked in the City, and she worked in marketing until she left to raise their three children. They'd never thought much about property, but in the mid-2000s housing boom with mortgages being dished out freely and everyone getting into buy-to-let, they decided to give it a go.

They discovered HMOs by chance after being shown around a house that was being used as one, and liked the idea. In January 2007 they found a house that was being sold with four tenants already in place. "We bought it from a lady of limited English who told us nothing except for giving us a scrap of paper showing how much each room was being rented for. We overpaid for the house, but the concept worked."

Soon afterwards they found another house, better value than the first, and they bought it with a 15% deposit. "It used to be let out as juvenile social housing, so it had boarded-up banisters to make sure they didn't hang themselves...that kind of thing." While her husband worked at his job in London, Serena spent three weeks painting and decorating while her baby son lay and played on the floor.

There was no great strategy, but the model worked. Soon though, her husband discovered 100% buy-to-let mortgages, and used them to expand their portfolio rapidly, buying houses all over the country with no real plan. One of their investments – the house where Serena now lives – was worth £187,500, but thanks to a dodgy surveyor they got a mortgage for £192,000. Their investment pot quickly dwindled, and the fees and refurb costs went onto credit cards.

For Serena's husband it was all about the gamble and the big picture, but she was more cautious – and having already done two refurbs on her own, she felt that she had a better understanding of what they were getting themselves into. "Apparently I wasn't being supportive and wasn't seeing the big picture. I had a small baby and two children at primary school at the time, and it's hard to fight against it when you've got kids nagging you, you've been up all night, and your husband is accusing you of not being ambitious – and all you've got to do is sign a bit of paper to make him stop."

It turned out that her husband had discovered not only 100% mortgages, but also spread-betting: he'd been racking up big gambling debts, while also finding the time to have an affair while living away from Serena and their kids during the week.

Soon after Serena found the bank statements and pieced everything together, they divorced.

Surveying the damage

By the time the buying spree had ended, Serena and her husband owned four houses in Eastbourne, one in Dartford, one in Leicester and three in Newcastle, with very little equity in any of them. "I know my exact loan-to-value across the portfolio because I had to work it out for the judge in the consent order...it's 92%. Not good."

Serena was given all the houses in the divorce, but they came along with £50,000 in credit card debt – a debt that had come to be known as the "refurbishment fund", but also included all manner of gambling debts and £3,000 fees for spread-betting courses. "I've paid off half of it out of my rental profits, but after all these years of work I've still not made anything for myself – I've just been paying off his debts."

Luckily she was given some money by her parents immediately after the divorce, which she used to move her family into one of their HMOs, ripping it back to brick and starting again. "Most people buy new boobs when they get divorced...I bought new shutters and doors." It cost £30,000, meaning she has £222,000 invested in a house that's not worth anything near that much. "But it's a nice place for my family to live. And I wouldn't have been able to rent anywhere with a cat, dog and two guinea pigs, and that's more important at the moment. It's all fine until interest rates go up, so it's on a repayment mortgage and I'm overpaying as much as I can."

She's now trying to sell off two of the properties outside Eastbourne to get the portfolio down to seven, and is taking on management of one of her new partner's HMOs to bring in more cash. "I feel trapped, but what else can I do? I've got one child at secondary school, two at primary school, all with different emotional needs and activities to be driven to. What other job could I do between 9am and 3pm except work in a school?"

"I'm probably a case study of how not to invest in property sensibly, but I'm the victim of someone who looked at the big picture and lost. I'm the one left living with it, and because I'm taking care of the details, I'm at least able to make a living out of it. Not a great living, but I'm making it work in a situation that could have bankrupted me."

Case study

Five-bedroom house in Eastbourne

Upfront expenses:

Purchase price: £170,000

Gross monthly rental income: £1732 (£80 per room per week)

Monthly expenses:

Mortgage: £300

Total bills: £550

Net monthly profit: £861

"If I was a hard bastard landlord flouting all the rules I could make a lot more money," Serena says, "but I wouldn't sleep so well."

She would also be making a lot more money if it wasn't for the situation she'd inherited: because of the 100% mortgages she started out with, the interest payments are far higher than they would have been with a more moderate level of leverage. "The mortgage on this house is £145,000, and it's probably worth £180,000 now. If I could ever pay it off, I'd be making £17,000 per year for doing virtually nothing except collecting the rent once a week. That's where you want to get to, and others have done it far more cleverly than me."

Serena's partner has followed her into HMO investing, and because it's been done more intentionally than hers he'll make more money more easily. "He bought at a great price, did all the work upfront, and put working people in there so he's not taking a risk on anyone. Even after paying me a management fee, he'll be making £1,000 per month without getting out of bed."

From the stories Serena tells about the situations with her tenants, it's clear that investors should never see the business of renting rooms to benefits recipients as an easy ride – and she says that they shouldn't be too blinded by the theoretical yield either. "You'll never get the maximum 15–20% you can get on paper because of maintenance, voids, unpaid rent and so on. Things *will* go wrong – they always do."

A peculiar bunch of tenants

Serena's relationship with her tenants is extraordinary, but it works. Even though she lends them money and cuts them a lot of slack, she collects 100% of the money she's owed in the end – although she sometimes has to wait for a tenant to come out of prison before she can get it.

Her tenants are a peculiar collection of individuals, but it's no accident who ends up in her houses. "I'm not trying to be Mother Theresa – I just believe that everyone should have the option of having a roof over their head, and I don't think it's possible for the government to help. It's down to us as individuals to help our fellow man, and I want to help people who I can have an honest working relationship with."

When she finds someone she senses she can take a chance on, she thinks carefully about where she can place them. "Each one of my houses has a different personality. One is full of foreign workers, where they don't talk to each other and they're fine with that. Another is going to become my OAP house, because they're all middle-aged and get on with each other in a weird kind of community of their own."

On her blog, Serena writes about some of her tenants – including Nadine, a woman with cancer who she drove to hospital appointments; Tom, a "friendly Rottweiler" who's an alcoholic; and Andrew, who grew up in care and has two brothers in prison.

Andrew phones while I'm talking to Serena, and she patiently talks him through incredibly basic tasks: working out how much money he has, who he needs to pay, and how to go to the council to get the forms he needs to re-start his benefits – he's just been fired from his job as a chef for threatening a waitress.

"When Andrew came to me he was selling keyrings on the street for a local gangster, and putting all his money into the slot machines in the arcade. He was only 22, had a son, was banned from all the local pubs for antisocial behaviour, and had a criminal conviction for holding up a bookie. He moved to Eastbourne in the first place to be with his mum – who rejected him yet again."

"He accepted all responsibility for what he'd done, and something about his honesty told me that I could take a chance on him. Even if it turns out he can't hack it, I'll be able to look at myself and say that I did everything I could."

She was given even more confidence in Andrew when there was a break-in at the house where he lived, and £1,200 in cash was stolen.

"Everyone – including me – accused Andrew, and I've never seen anyone fight so hard to clear his name. I realised I was just as guilty as anyone else of assuming it was him because of his history. In the end, it turned out that another tenant staged the break-in to 'steal' the money because he owed it to a gangster."

A practical approach

Serena's approach to management is as hands-on as it gets – her phone is always ringing, and she has no choice but to live locally because of the frequent call-outs. "Self-closing bloody doors! I got three callouts last night, all because of doors."

This management style is essential though: because she has such large interest payments as a result of the loan-to-value of her portfolio being so high, she couldn't afford to have empty rooms or uncollected rent.

Her Saturday morning in-person rent collections started as a necessity because it was the only way she could be sure of getting her money, but she now credits them with solving a lot of problems before they appear. "It takes me three hours to do the rounds sometimes, but it's worth it – we have a ten-minute chat, it's amazing what I can find out. They become friends too – we'll have a coffee and a catch-up, which helps me to find out what's important to them. They're the weirdest friends I've ever had, but friends all the same!"

If she can't collect rent from someone and they're not responding to her, she'll just set up camp outside their room. "It's very funny when they come in at 3am and find me reading a book outside their door. They're so stunned that they can't come up with any excuses on the spot, and we work something out."

When relationships become less friendly, she takes a pragmatic view. "Lots of my tenants are exceptionally manipulative, because they've grown up in care and it's the only way they've been able to survive. I have to be very black-and-white: 'I'm not your mother and I'm not your girlfriend, and you can't use emotional blackmail with me.' In many cases it's the first time a woman's ever been straight with them."

Often, it's a blip that will improve Serena's relationship with a tenant. "When something goes wrong, they expect me to come around ranting and raving and accusing them of all sorts. I just say to them, 'You've been an idiot, you've screwed up. Now, what are we going to do about it?' That makes them trust me and realise that I'm really not out to get them."

Sometimes though, situations can't be salvaged. She'll give them options: she can either serve a Section 21 notice and take them to court, or give the police a key to the communal areas, or give them money to go away. "When I ask someone to leave, it has to be on good terms because I'm going to see these people around town when I'm out with my kids. If I give them options, I've given them control so they can't possibly be aggrieved."

The most money she's ever paid someone to leave is £500. "He was a Viagra dealer, and he just *had* to leave because he was upsetting everyone so much they were locking themselves in their rooms. He was even threatening me in front of the police. He wanted £1,000 to leave, but I offered him £500 because it's what I had on me, and as I was walking away he took it. Twenty minutes later he was gone.

For him it's the most money he's going to see in a long time, and for me it was a small price to get rid of a big problem."

It sounds like she regularly puts herself into situations that others wouldn't consider safe, but "I don't scare easily – I used to, but I quickly worked out that if someone's ranting and raving it's invariably because of some other issue they're going through, and it's not really about me. Also, being a woman in this job is advantageous because if they're going to have a fight they won't do it in front of me, and it'd take a lot for them to hit me."

An infinite market

Although it seems risky to have tenants who can behave unpredictably and are hard work to collect rent from, the demand at least is as risk-free as it gets: "It's an infinite market, and it'll never go away. It's just a case of selecting the right people out of that infinite market."

"We all want doctors and pharmacists and airline pilots as tenants, but we're never going to get them because they've got their own houses. You're always going to end up with the slightly odd people at the bottom, but the odd people at the bottom can be more reliable than the people at the top. I've got my own example of that – my ex-husband was in the top 1% of the earning population and he screwed me royally, whereas the bottom end of society has rarely screwed me over."

Serena also believes that the HMO model is less risky than many other investments because the risk of non-payment is spread between five or six tenants. "Take my own house – it'd rent for £850 per month to a family, so that's what I'd lose if they didn't pay me.

It'd take a hell of a long time for one of my guys to build up £850 of arrears, and by then I'd have had a chance to do something about it. I did have one tenant who ended up £900 in arrears – he'd been sentenced to three months in prison, and I thought he'd just gone to work in London – but we worked it out, and now he only owes me £50."

The benefits system

Rather than blaming the tenants, Serena believes that a lot of the problems she encounters are a result of how the benefits system is set up.

"It used to be a great system – at the start of a claim they'd be given a cheque payable to me for four weeks' rent, and I'd get paid directly by the council after that. Brilliant – everyone got what they wanted."

"Then LHA came in, and suddenly a tenant with nothing to their name would get £400 dumped into their bank account. I'd not get paid, the tenant would be in the pub and the council wouldn't discuss the case with me. I understand that they're trying to give people responsibility for their finances, but it's not much good for anyone when you're dealing with vulnerable people."

"I'm glad I don't run the government, because I don't have an answer to any of it. There needs to be a safety net, but there needs to be an incentive to work too: I see a certain amount of laziness in my lot that's been bred into them by the system, but some people are just vulnerable and need help. The government needs to read *Animal Farm* – we're not all created equal, and that's what makes the human race so interesting."

The future

For now, Serena is happy providing a service to her motley crew of tenants. She's considering taking on the management for other investors, but knows that her approach won't scale too far. "I saw a job advertised for a letting agent and I was tempted, but I know I'd spend all day having to fob people off after other people's mistakes and I couldn't hack it."

If she had the money, her dream would be to set up a home for people who'd just come out of prison: they'd learn how to be good tenants, build up some credibility, and learn very basic skills like how to do the washing and keep their room tidy. "A lot of people who've never lived in a safe environment just don't know how to deal with it. It'd work: it'd make money and reduce reoffending...but it'd take half a million quid, so it's not going to happen."

In the meantime, she's written her first book and is starting on the second. "I always wanted to be a journalist, so the writing is my way of getting to use a bit more creativity than I do with the houses."

Asked whether, given the choice, she'd rather have working tenants who were less effort and still make the same amount of money, she says she'd rather keep her current lot. "I do get exhausted, and I do get fed up, but they're interesting people and I feel like I can help them."

"And besides," she says, "it gives me something to write about."

Lessons

For long-term investments, look for signs of long-lasting demand

There will always be a demand for Edwardian/Victorian terraces, and there won't be a shortage of people needing to rent rooms. Demographic trends point to people making a lifestyle choice to rent a room for a fixed price rather than stretch themselves by getting their own flat, and the number of single-person households is on the rise.

You need to have control

Even if you've got an agent managing a property, you need to make sure the tenant knows who you are in case the agent's not doing their job and they need to tell you. "I always send a box of biscuits at Christmas with my name and phone number so they can get hold of me if they need me. You just need to make sure it'll go through the letterbox!"

Think about what *type* of risk you're comfortable with

Serena's taking on a fair amount of personal risk and hassle, but she'll never face the problem of not being able to find a steady stream of new tenants. She has a reasonable risk of non-payment, but as there are five or six people in a house, one non-payer will never be catastrophic. There are different types of risk, and it's a personal decision as to which type you can accept.

Details matter

Serena's ex-husband only cared about the big picture, but "In property, it's the details that'll stop you." It's exciting to sit calculating yields and making big projections, but you need to have plans for dealing with the nuts and bolts too.

Leverage can come at the expense of cashflow

Serena would love to have 50% loan-to-value across her portfolio, because the reduced interest payments would mean she'd be making a significantly greater profit each month. It would also give her more options: she can't sell her houses because there's no cash in them, and she'd be losing her income stream.

Treat tenants fairly, and they'll cause fewer problems

Serena is always calm and factual with her tenants, making it hard for them to be aggrieved even if she's asking them to leave. She'll always say "We need to talk about your behaviour the other day" or "We need to talk about your tenancy," never "We need to talk about you." If she feels unsafe she'll bring a friend with her, but then she'll insist that the tenant brings a friend too so it's not two against one. She gives them options so they feel like they have a say in the outcome.

Conclusion

Even before I wrote this book, I'd had a few years of spending a lot of time with investors. And one thing gradually became clear to me: there are almost as many paths to success in property as there are individual investors.

Portfolios can be built fast or slow, near to or far from home, made up of small flats for professionals, large shared houses for those on the breadline, and everything in between.

And that realisation is what prompted this book in the first place: if the exact strategy you use doesn't predict success or failure, what does? Going beyond the bricks, is there some characteristic of the person that predicts success?

This chapter will aim to do two things:

Sum up my observations about the similarities and differences between our group of investors in terms of their backgrounds and personalities

Look at how their chosen investment strategies were informed by their attitudes and lifestyles

Origins

If we went back and met each investor at the age of 18, would we be able to predict that they would have made a mark in property – or indeed outside the world of the 9-to-5 in general?

If you were to pick out one, it would probably be Gavin – his childhood entrepreneurial exploits indicate that he was never destined for cubicle life. There's also Arsh, who had little choice but to get involved in his father's business young, and who you therefore might have suspected would end up running the whole thing. And Mat, who was clearly suited to entrepreneurship if he could nudge his schemes onto the right side of the law.

At the other end of the spectrum, Nichola was about to start training in social work, Lisa was about to discover a career that kept her extremely satisfied for over a decade, and Jonathan didn't seem particularly inclined to do anything until he discovered that police work suited him well.

The group isn't united by academic performance either. Three of them went to university, which is probably about typical given their ages, while Kim and Mark struggled at school and left as early as they could. None of them were marked out as being unusually intelligent, although all are sharp and display a real curiosity about the people and the world around them.

If the group had anything in common, it would have been a drive to do their own thing – even if that was completely unrelated to business. Kim was dedicated to martial arts, and Mark was heavily into breakdancing. Lisa was scaling every barrier to becoming a pilot, and Nichola was planning her escape to the other side of the world. That drive to do something different from their peers will have served them well when the opportunity came to do something that most other people don't do: work for themselves, take risks, and build success on an ability to spot opportunities that most people never identify.

What got them started?

The group is similarly diverse when it comes to the push that first got them started in property – with only Gavin making the deliberate decision to pursue property as a route to wealth relatively young, after considering all his other options.

Mark and Jonathan could both be classed as "accidental landlords", who eventually came to appreciate the benefits of renting out property. Mark was forced by circumstance to rent out his own home, while Jonathan was in a position to buy a new family home while hanging onto his old one – but in both cases it was many years until they returned to property in a more deliberate way, and seriously made up for lost time.

Others discovered property very suddenly. Nichola and Lisa were both gnawingly aware that their careers wouldn't give them the freedom and lifestyle they wanted, but had no idea what the answer was – until out of nowhere, a single factor (a leaflet and a book respectively) appeared at exactly the right time to turn them towards property.

Mat's story had both aspects. He spent years as an accidental landlord of one property, but sold it without a second thought before he received his own bolt from the blue: a forced relocation to Aberdeen, which just happened to be the best place in the UK to invest in property at the time, combined with a chance glance at an estate agent's window that led to his moment of insight.

Serena and Arsh both had their initial portfolios forced upon them – albeit in very different circumstances. Both of them took something that was working to an extent, and changed the model to create a more profitable, sustainable business out of what they were given.

Hard work and doing things properly

However they got started, and however ambitious they are regarding the size of their portfolio and how much money they want to make, almost every investor works exceptionally hard on their business. They live in a blur of phone calls, emails, viewings and meetings…and they thrive on it.

The exceptions are Jonathan, Mat and Mark, who all claim not to do very much these days. Yet Mat is still building his portfolio at quite a clip, and it seems like he just enjoys his work so much that he's not always aware that he's doing it. Mark and Jonathan might not be so active now, but they were clearly exceptionally driven to build up large portfolios alongside their day jobs – and both devote a hefty chunk of their free time to discussing property online and helping others.

Alongside the hard work is a clear desire to do the right thing by their tenants – treating them as "customers", even in the most difficult of circumstances. Arsh and Serena both have tenant markets that can be exceptionally challenging, and frequently find that their trust and respect isn't repaid – but both passionately defend their tenants when anyone tries to do them down.

In every case, however the investor runs their business, the end result for the tenant is a good service. While Lisa runs the administrative side of her business meticulously and Kim is more chaotic, neither would allow a tenant's problem to go unresolved. The same goes for Jonathan, who'd cheerfully pop round to fix the problem himself, and Mat, who would quickly ditch a letting agent who didn't do it for him.

Investment criteria

Of all the investors, it was probably only Mat who started out with a firm plan for what he would and wouldn't invest in: he knew how much money he wanted to make, how many properties he would need to get him there, and he distilled everything down to a yield number that underpinned his whole plan. Even Mat's approach evolved over time though, as he came to realise that capital growth had vastly outstripped the income he had actually been targeting.

All of the other investors started without a strict set of criteria, and to a greater or lesser extent have refined their approach over the years. Mark, for example, started by buying almost anything, but now focuses on investing in a particular type of bungalow plot where he knows he can add significant value. Jonathan never strayed from standard buy-to-let, but it took a while for him to identify the LHA market and work out exactly how much he should be paying for a property to give him his targeted 25% ROI. Gavin dabbled in various different types of property, before settling on student houses with more than five bedrooms where he can make a return on investment of 25% and a net profit of at least £1,000 per month. He has even more detailed criteria for the properties themselves – two social spaces and equal sized bedrooms – because he has discovered that these characteristics reduce conflict and make for longer tenancies.

Others have a preferred type of property or target market, but take a flexible approach and will take on a good deal of any type if they spot one. Nichola, for example, is open to doing any kind of creative deal if it solves a problem for the people involved – even if it doesn't immediately make her a significant return. Lisa likes to buy ex-council houses which will rent easily to professional tenants, but she's bought all kinds of different properties with all manner of strategies because she spotted an opportunity.

It's not at all surprising that most of the investors started out without a firm plan: most people start out in property by just buying a second property as the opportunity arises; it's only as they gain experience that they realise what works and what's possible. However, it's probably worth noting that the investors who achieved their goals the fastest (Gavin and Mat) were also the most intentional in their approach. We can probably conclude that having a firm plan and taking fast, decisive action is desirable – but we can also be reassured that starting with the end in mind isn't a prerequisite for success.

Risk tolerance

Of course, every investor takes risks – and in most cases it's impossible to say whether one approach is definitively riskier than another. What is interesting, though, is the *type* of risk that different investors perceive.

Many people, for example, see the LHA market as being exceptionally risky. They see a tenant market that can need a lot of support, who have limited disincentives for not paying their rent, and an income stream that's contingent on the bureaucratic vagaries of the local authority.

But the likes of Arsh, Serena and Jonathan have built their entire businesses around this market. Each of them separately referred to the benefits of a "near-infinite market": they know that if they have properties that are of a high standard and competitively priced, they will never struggle to attract a large pool of tenants from whom they can take their pick. They have developed systems to manage the risks and challenges of the LHA market, and now they would perceive it as far more risky to own a big, detached house suitable for professionals – what if there's a period of time when a professional family who can afford the rent can't be found?

There is a similar argument around the issue of single lets versus HMOs. Lisa, Mark and Mat see HMOs as too much work, with a high risk of voids, conflicts and damage. However, Serena and Kim have come to prefer HMOs because they perceive them as being less risky – if one tenant in a five-bedroom house doesn't pay, they lose 20% of their income rather than 100% if a non-paying family occupied the same house.

With both of these debates, there's no right or wrong – but the passionate opinions on each side (each thinking the other is slightly mad) show the extent to which a strategy in property should depend on personal attitudes rather than just blindly trying to replicate someone else's successful model.

One type of risk in which our group is more united is their attitude to debt. Whereas most people would typically think of debt as bad and try to pay off their mortgage as quickly as possible, these investors see debt as the most powerful tool they have. Even those who experienced the sky-high interest rates of the early 90s have little hesitation in borrowing as much money as they can, knowing that it holds the key to growing their portfolio and generating more income. Only Gavin specifically mentioned being worried about the level of debt within his portfolio and was taking decisive action to pay it down to a level he was more comfortable with.

There are some differences within the group when it comes to debt, though. Mark has a fairly unique position, in that he borrows as much as he possibly can but also carries far higher cash reserves than anyone else. He believes that borrowing the maximum at all times is a way to transfer risk from himself to the lender – but he still wants to hold plenty of cash to ride out any storms, and to put himself in a position to take advantage if the economy slumps again.

Jonathan takes the opposite position on cash reserves, arguing that his money is best used in buying more properties to generate yet more income, and if push comes to shove he could raise £100,000 to pay for any unforeseen expenses relatively easily. Lisa is in a unique position to see what's working for other investors, and to her it looks like those who are doing the best (and who are sleeping best) are those with relatively low levels of debt who sat out the boom and only started buying again when prices fell.

Where to buy?

Another interesting point of comparison is where each person has chosen to buy: have they stuck to their local area, or gone further afield?

Most of our investors have stuck near to where they live, either by design or circumstance. Serena's management style means that she has no choice but to have her investment around the corner from her house. Jonathan is lucky enough to live in an area that has excellent investing potential, but you sense that he wouldn't start investing three hours away from home whatever the numbers told him. Lisa meanwhile has no particular objection to owning properties anywhere, but believes that she can make better investments where she has strong local knowledge – and likes being able to nip problems in the bud by inspecting properties herself between tenancies.

Others have taken a different approach. Gavin and Nichola originally lived in London, and recognised that it wasn't the place for a new investor with limited funds to be starting out. Both still wanted to take a hands-on approach, so took the drastic step of moving themselves to the other end of the country – they still invested close to home, but changed where "home" was. Perhaps they had weaker ties as both moved to London from other countries originally, but their commitment is nevertheless impressive. Mark, meanwhile, started locally then leveraged his family connections to put himself in a position to buy good deals wherever in the country they happen to be.

Mat is the only one of our investors who actually turns over his portfolio based on where he sees the opportunity as being for the next few years. He started in Aberdeen, refinanced to build a second portfolio in Germany, and is now selling everything in Germany to move his portfolio back to different parts of the UK. He gives some consideration to how easy it will be for him to spend time on the ground in the places where he could potentially invest, but for the most part he operates more like an institutional investor than a private one: identifying global opportunities, swooping, then letting other people manage while he keeps an eye out for the signs that he should be selling up and moving on.

Exit strategy

The exit strategies of the group are fairly evenly split between the only two things you can do: sell up and cash in, or hold the properties for income and pass them on to children.

Several of the interviewees expressed a desire for greater simplicity as time goes on. Lisa's plan is to end up with 10–12 unencumbered properties making £750 each, so that she can have a well-funded retirement with little to worry about. Gavin is already striving to pay down his debt to a more manageable level, and Mark is flirting with the fantasy of selling everything and moving abroad.

In many cases, the investors are putting a lot of emphasis on removing themselves from the running of the business. Arsh, Nichola, Mark, Kim and Gavin have all been setting up agencies that can run their portfolios in their absence – and can generate extra revenue by using the same systems to manage properties for other investors.

Luck?

Before ending, I should attempt to answer a question that some readers will undoubtedly be asking: have these investors just been lucky?

To a large extent, of course they have – as they are the first to admit. They have all lived in a country at a time when conditions have been broadly favourable for property investment, and even the recent recession didn't cause a spike in interest rates that could have caused significant problems.

But then, millions of other people lived in these same conditions – people who never invested at all, or were put off by an early bad experience, or who pushed it too far and lost everything. And everyone in this book has encountered some kind of personal challenge that could easily have led to them throwing in the towel.

So some degree of luck is probably necessary to have success in property investment (or indeed in anything), but it isn't sufficient. The investors we've met have found success by combining their luck with tenacity, dedication, a willingness to take risks, and an uncommon amount of common sense.

The "Are they just lucky?" question is a reasonable one to ask, but only becomes damaging when it's used as an excuse for being unwilling to try to replicate their results. There are plenty of less lucky people in the world, but there are some who are more lucky too. There have been worse times to invest in property, but there have been better.

What marks out these particular investors is that they've taken the small amount they've started with, and worked with the situations they've been given to end up with lives that they love and financial security that most could (and do) only dream of.

Lifestyle

While many of the investors need never work again if they don't want to, none of them is sitting idle.

Everyone in the group, to a greater or lesser extent, has systems in place that allows their business to run with limited involvement from them – they just choose to use this freedom of time in different ways.

Gavin, for example, has systems that allow him to do even more. By delegating the management of all his properties, he's able to dabble in developments, sourcing, teaching and all manner of other projects. Mark, meanwhile, has systems that allow him to do less, but he still chooses to spend his free time involved in property – even if not on his own portfolio.

The least systematic of the group are probably Jonathan and Serena – although this in itself is a lifestyle choice. Jonathan could outsource the management of all his properties to an outside company, take a 15% hit on his income, and never need to work again – but he enjoys the sociability of visiting his tenants and the satisfaction of solving their problems far too much to let someone else do it, let alone to pay them for doing so.

Serena's tenant market is such that it couldn't be so easily delegated, and it's her hands-on, personal approach that has allowed her to support her family with her business rather than it becoming the huge liability it could have been. But she clearly gets her satisfaction from helping her tenants too – and admits that if she had the money, she'd provide accommodation to offenders who had just come out of prison.

Mat has long been at a point where he doesn't need to work, and Arsh is planning to be at that point inside ten years. Arsh admits that rather than retiring he'd probably just start another business, and Mat looked horrified when I pointed out that he could just leave his portfolio as it is and step back a bit. Even Nichola, who worked herself into a position where she could take her son back to

New Zealand for an extended stay, admits that she's spending a lot of time out on research trips while she's out there.

Whether this busy lifestyle is chosen (like Mat) or forced by current circumstances (like Kim), you sense that they wouldn't have it any other way. It's probably largely due to this restlessness and drive that they were successful in the first place, and it's not something they can just turn off now.

Although you'll have seen from reading their stories that some of the investors enjoy more "flashy" material lifestyles than others, none of them seem to derive their pleasure from their physical possessions or the experiences their money can buy. Rather, all of these people have found a way of life where they can do work they enjoy, set themselves up for a secure financial future, and do it all with complete autonomy.

They haven't taken the easy path, but they would all agree that the journey has been worth it.

Now get your exclusive bonuses!

If you've got all the way to the end and still want more, I'd like to send you a few little extras to say thank you!

Firstly, I've put together a handy 3-step guide to choosing your ideal property strategy. If you've read about all the approaches in this book and you're still not sure which is right for you, this should really help.

I've also get extra notes on two of my favourite chapters that I couldn't fit into the book.

They're yours for free – all I need is your email address so I know where to send them.

Register for the bonuses here: www.propertygeek.net/btb

Acknowledgements

The inspiration for this book came from the excellent *Free Capital* by Guy Thomas, which contains a series of interviews with private investors who've become "ISA millionaires". It's a fascinating read if you have even the most passing of interests in stock market investing. .

Guy gave me his blessing to rip off / "take inspiration from" his format, and provided generous suggestions and encouragement throughout the process.

I'm also grateful to my editor (who happens to be my wife), without whom that last clause would have said "Im all so greatful too my editor". I also had no idea just how many ways it was possible to inconsistently write "buy to let/buy-to-let/Buy to Let" until she pointed it out. Forcefully.

My greatest thanks, though, have to be reserved for the interviewees in this book. They gave up several hours of their time, patiently corrected the glaring factual errors in my first draft, and told their stories with openness, honesty and humour. The stories of these "everyday" investors were just as inspirational and insightful as I imagined they would be when I was planning this book, and I hope I've served them well.

Also by this author: *Property Investment for Beginners*

Even though spiralling prices are a thing of the past, you're still convinced property could be your key to financial freedom.

And it could. But where do you start? Do you invest near where you live, or wherever yields are best? Do you rent to families, or professionals, or students? Should you be trawling through Rightmove or lurking at property auctions?

This short book covers the big questions you should be asking yourself before you so much as glance at an estate agent's window. It contains a jargon-free explanation of basic investment principles, summaries of the major post-crunch investment strategies, and advice on developing a mindset that will support your long-term success.

You'll learn...

- How to pick an investment strategy that matches your skills and goals

- The only three calculations you need to know to size up any deal

- An overview of every major investment approach, from the most boring to the probably-not-a-good-idea-but-here-you-go-anyway

- How to (safely and sustainably) stretch a limited pot of cash to build whatever size portfolio you want

...although you will need to endure some pretty shocking jokes along the way. Sorry about that.

Buy *Property Investment for Beginners* on Amazon now: www.propertygeek.net/buybeginners

Glossary

Below market value (BMV)

Buying a property for less than it's worth. The most common reasons for being able to buy BMV are a vendor who is under pressure to sell quickly, or a property that needs significant refurbishment and is scaring off potential buyers.

Determining what the market value of a property "should" be is based on finding comparable properties nearby that have sold recently.

Bridging

A specialist form of short-term financing, which normally has high interest rates compared to mortgages. It is often used for purchases at auction (where there isn't time to arrange a mortgage), on properties that are unmortgageable for some reason (often because they aren't inhabitable at the time of purchase), or where the investor is planning on selling the property quickly.

Bridging finance is subdivided into "closed bridging" (where a firm payback date is set when taking out the loan) and "open bridging" (where there is no set date for paying it back – although it is still usually within a certain timeframe)..

Buy-to-let (BTL)

Buying a property for the purpose of renting it out to someone else rather than living there yourself. The term itself was invented by the Association of Residential Letting Agents (ARLA) in 1995, with the creation of specialist buy-to-let mortgages. Prior to that, commercial financing arrangements were the only way to buy property as an investment.

Buy-to-sell

Buying a house with the aim of selling it on for a profit, without renting it out first.

Capital growth / capital appreciation

The difference between what a property was worth at one point in time versus what it is worth at a future point. For example, if a property was worth £100,000 when you bought it and £150,000 when you sold it, you would have benefited from capital growth or capital appreciation of £50,000. It can also be expressed as a percentage, so in our example there would have been capital growth of 50%.

Capital value

The market price of a property. The market price can never truly be known until it is sold, but it can be estimated by using comparable properties in the local area that have been sold recently.

Cash purchase

Buying a property without taking out a mortgage on it. A purchase still counts as being made in cash if the money was raised by taking out a mortgage on a different property.

House in multiple occupation (HMO)

Also known as "House of multiple occupancy".

Broadly, a property in which three or more people form two or more households, and who share a kitchen or bathroom. A "household" is defined as "members of the same family", and includes people who are married or living together as a couple.

For example, two students sharing a house would not count as an HMO (not three or more people), and nor would a family of five (only one household).

For a more comprehensive definition, see www.nationalhmonetwork.com/definition.php.

Lease option

A type of contract where both parties agree that at the end of a set rental period, the renter will have the option (but not the obligation) to buy the property at a prearranged price.

In most cases, including the instances in this book, an investor will rent the property to a tenant during the option period rather than living there themselves. They might also choose to "assign" their option to the tenant for a fee, so the tenant can choose to buy it directly from the owner without the investor needing to have any period of ownership.

Loan-to-value (LTV)

The amount of money borrowed as a percentage of the asset it is secured against. For example, if you took out a mortgage of £75,000 to buy a house worth £100,000, your mortgage would have a loan-to-value of 75%.

Local Housing Allowance (LHA)

A method of calculating the level of housing benefit that tenants are entitled to for renting private accommodation. The term "LHA market" is often used to describe all tenants who are in receipt of housing benefit.

The country is divided into Broad Rental Market Areas (BRMA), and within each area a set level of housing benefit is paid depending on the number of bedrooms a claimant is entitled to. The bedroom entitlement is determined by the size and composition of the family claiming.

The level of rent for each number of bedrooms in each BRMA is intended to give housing benefit claimants access to roughly the cheapest 30% of private homes which are offered for rent.

Under the LHA scheme, benefits are paid directly to the claimant, and it is their responsibility to pay the rent to the landlord. It is possible for the landlord to be paid directly if the tenant is classed as "vulnerable" or falls more than eight weeks into arrears.

Mortgage Express

A mortgage lender which was very active prior to the credit crunch, and went bust soon after. It is now being run by the government until it is able to redeem all its loans so it can officially close down.

It was one of the most permissive lenders, allowing "self-certification" mortgages with very few checks on the borrower, and "same-day refinancing" (defined later).

Off-plan

Property which has not yet been built, or is in the process of being built. The developer often offers a discount as an incentive for the buyer to take the risk of buying before the property is finished, because it provides them with revenue without having to wait for construction to be complete.

Rent-to-rent

The business model of renting out a whole property from its owner, and sub-letting it room by room. Profit is made because renting rooms individually tends to produce a higher rental income.

Rent-to-rent must be done with the full knowledge of the property owner, and after taking specialist legal advice to make sure the correct contracts are in place. If an HMO is created, local regulations must be abided by too.

Return on investment

The annual income from a property, after all costs, expressed as a percentage of the amount of money that was put into the deal by the investor.

For example, you buy a property worth £100,000 by putting in £25,000 and taking out a 75% LTV mortgage. You spend £15,000 on furnishings and legal fees.

Your personal investment is therefore £40,000. If the property generates an annual income of £5,000 after all costs (including mortgage payments, agency fees, repairs etc), their return on investment is 12.5% (£5,000 divided by £40,000).

Same-day refinancing

Also known as "no money down" and "instant remortgaging".

Before the credit crunch, some lenders would allow you to buy a property using bridging finance (see above for a definition of this) and instantly remortgage for 85% of the property's value. If you could buy a property for £85,000 and get it independently valued at £100,000, the mortgage lender would therefore lend you £85,000. You could use that £85,000 to repay the bridging loan (which you would only need for a few hours), and you would own a property having used none of your own money.

This practice was ended through the introduction of tougher valuation and lending criteria, and the enforcing of a guideline that stated that someone must own a property for six months before being able to remortgage.

Stamp duty

Short for Stamp Duty Land Tax. This is a tax on property transactions where the buyer has to pay a percentage of the purchase price to HMRC. At the time of publication there is no stamp duty payable on purchases under £125,000, 1% on purchases up to £250,000, and higher percentages for more expensive purchases.

The stamp duty threshold is important because you would pay no stamp duty on a purchase of £124,000, but £1,260 on a purchase of £126,000.

Universal Credit

A new welfare benefit that will combine and replace six other payments – including housing benefit. A pilot scheme was due to begin in April 2013, but as of early 2014 its roll-out has been very limited due to IT problems.

The key element for property investors is that housing benefit will now be included in Universal Credit, and it will be more difficult for landlords to receive the payment directly from the local authority – because the housing benefit isn't a separate payment that can just be re-routed. There will also be a cap to the overall level of benefit that a family can claim, which might leave them without enough money to pay their rent.

The subject has attracted much concern and speculation since it was first announced in 2012, but its true impact on property investors is not yet known.

Vendor financing

An umbrella term for methods of purchasing a property that include lease options, instalment contracts and delayed completion. The common element is that the vendor offers some kind of "payment terms", so that the investor doesn't have to buy outright with cash or a mortgage. Popular "payment terms" include the option for the investor to pay in instalments; and the option for the investor to make full payment at a set date in the future rather than right away.

These techniques allow investors to do deals that would not otherwise be possible. They're sometimes considered controversial because they involve complex legal arrangements that vendors might struggle to fully understand the risks of.

Yield

The annual income that a property generates, as a proportion of its capital value.

"Gross yield" involves dividing the rental income by its capital value. For example, a property worth £100,000 that commands an annual rent of £7,500 would give a gross yield of 7.5%

"Net yield" is calculated by deducting all costs from the rental income before dividing it by the capital value. In the above example, if there were costs of £5,000 (from mortgage payments, agency fees etc), the net rental income would be £2,500. This would give a net yield of 2.5%.

Printed in Great Britain
by Amazon